OSCAR OF BETWEEN

OSCAR
of BETWEEN

A Memoir of Identity and Ideas

BETSY WARLAND

[signature]

Dagger EDITIONS

AN IMPRINT OF

CAITLIN PRESS

Caitlin Press Inc.
8100 Alderwood Road, Halfmoon Bay, BC V0N 1Y1
www.caitlin-press.com

Edited by Barbara Kuhne
Text and cover design by Vici Johnstone
Cover image shutterstock_91134623
Printed in Canada

Caitlin Press Inc. acknowledges financial support from the Government of
Canada and the Canada Council for the Arts, and from the Province of British
Columbia through the British Columbia Arts Council and the Book Publisher's
Tax Credit.

 Canada Council **Conseil des Arts**
for the Arts **du Canada**

 BRITISH COLUMBIA
ARTS COUNCIL
We acknowledge the support of the Province of British Columbia
through the British Columbia Arts Council

Library and Archives Canada Cataloguing in Publication

Warland, Betsy, 1946-, author

Oscar of between : a memoir of identity and ideas / Betsy Warland.

ISBN 978-1-987915-16-7 (paperback)

1. Warland, Betsy, 1946-. 2. Gender identity. 3. Authors, Canadian

(English)—20th century—Biography. I. Title.

PS8595.A7745Z53 2016   C811'.54   C2015-908100-9

Other Books by Betsy Warland

Breathing the Page: Reading the Act of Writing (essays). Toronto: Cormorant Books, 2010.

Only This Blue (long poem and essay). Toronto: The Mercury Press, 2005.

Bloodroot: Tracing the Untelling of Motherloss (memoir). Toronto: Second Story Press, 2000.

What Holds Us Here (poetry). Ottawa: Buschek Books, 1998.

Two Women in a Birth (poetry and prose with Daphne Marlatt). Toronto: Guernica Editions, 1994.

The Bat Had Blue Eyes (poetry and prose). Toronto: Women's Press, 1993.

Proper Deafinitions (creative nonfiction). Vancouver: Press Gang Publishers, 1990.

Double Negative (poetry and prose with Daphne Marlatt). Charlottetown: gynergy books/Ragweed Press, 1988.

serpent (w)rite (a long poem). Toronto: Coach House Press, 1987.

open is broken (poetry). Edmonton: Longspoon Press, 1984.

A Gathering Instinct (poetry). Toronto: Williams-Wallace, 1981.

Contents

Author's Note

Oscar of Between began when I flew to London in 2007 to celebrate my sixtieth birthday. As a complete draft of *Breathing the Page: Reading the Act of Writing* (2010) was in sight, I could entertain what my next manuscript might be. On the flight, I realized I wanted to combine the personal essay style of ideas used in *Breathing the Page* with the memoir style and form I used in *Bloodroot: Tracing the Untelling of Motherloss* (2000). However, I wanted to challenge myself with one new wild card: the use of one fictive device. Once in London, I followed an odd compulsion to see the *Camouflage* exhibit in the Imperial War Museum.

There I experienced a revelation, and I was off and running. From the beginning, I reserved judgement as to whether *Oscar of Between* would ever be a print book. Although I adore print books, I had become disenchanted by my five-year-long experience of being turned down by publishers who loved *Breathing the Page* but whose marketing departments nixed it. So, I just enjoyed writing *Oscar of Between* for a number of years. In 2012, I got the idea of creating an online Oscar's Salon, where I could publish short excerpts from an abridged version of the manuscript; curate a wide variety of Guest Writers or Artists who would send me a piece of their work that bounced off mine; and re-activate my visual art training and incorporate images. In addition, I invited readers to post their comments. I relished salon readers' riffs, creative responses and insights that weren't critiques, book blurbs, reviews nor blog opinion posts. They struck me as a kind of new sub-genre form. Oscar's Salon felt (and continues to feel) as close as I could get to "real time" exchanges with an audience, readers, and with sister and fellow creators.

In March of 2015, I wrote the final part of *Oscar of Between*, read the entire manuscript for the first time, and realized it should be a print book too. I posted a comment on the salon and indicated I wanted to have it published within a year so that it could interact with Oscar's Salon. In today's publishing world, this timeline was almost unheard of, but a staff member of Caitlin Press (who had been following the salon) emailed me and asked if I would be interested in meeting with her publisher. I am pleased to say it's a good fit, and the complete book is in your hands a year later.

Oscar's Salon at www.betsywarland.com/excerpts-from-oscar-of-between will be live with monthly postings until early fall of 2016 and will remain up after it is finished. I urge you to travel the arc between book and digital salon as each possesses it own vitality, surprise, appeal.

Betsy Warland
Vancouver, BC

Part 1

London, Vancouver, Iowa 2007

Oscar.

Inexplicably entering the Imperial War Museum. London.
30.3.07. Sodden gusting air (outside). Atmospheric twilight of
Camouflage Exhibit (inside). Oscar, having quickly walked by
permanent collection (its secrets intact).

Oscar.

Last time travelled alone: 1992. Amsterdam. Wrote the Van
Gogh suite:
                "to see so vividly &   not be seen."

Oscar.

Now rummaging through satchel for ear-length pencil. On
exhibition ticket
scribbling quote from first display case:

"Art alone could screen men and intentions where natural
cover failed."

S. J. Solomon
British artist and camouflage officer

Oscar
: neither man,
nor marked with natural cover.

That leaves her
with art.

First display case. Dumbstruck. For all her notable difference, this one had eluded Oscar. This unidentified force. Shaping her life. Had thought it had nothing to do — with her. Until. This moment.

Camouflage
: necessity of.

Oscar
: lack of.

Oscar at odds.

Bewilderment exiting her body — last grains in hourglass — gasp.

Sixty years to get here.

– 3 –

"At a slant." Dickinson knew. Glimpses of a narrative's ghosts. Most a writer can hope for.

– 4 –

In the deep of night — swell of sadness.
Oscar's son. Absence. Asunder. Ache of it. In the wake of numerous challenges, survival instincts intensify: devotion is not enough. After seven years, determined. Done. Only one real mother." Done. How could? It was. Is. Will be. Oscar. Two provinces away. Training herself. To change *without* him. To *with* her self.

In restaurants: "How many?"

"Just — one."

-5-

Brenda Hillman: " ... the word and the sentence share custody of the phrase." Her young daughter "ferrying" back and forth. No more mom and dad. (Now you have TWO homes!)

Hillman
: " ... my writing was falling apart." Rupture everywhere.

The sentence in denial.

Word and phrase make do.

-6-

Oscar. Drying. Her then three-year-old son walked in. To pee. Peering. Expecting a penis. On her. Trying to make sense of it. He signed: "You're my dad." Began after Oscar's surgery. Double mastectomy. Oscar more than ever in between.

Familiar to Oscar.

Bewildering to her son.
Him just getting boys and girls.

Oscar. Addressed as "Sir" and "Ma'am" within seconds. Membership is how it works. Automatic positioning. What to expect. Who to trust. And not.

Her son bewilders others too. "What's that thing on his ear?" Him between normal and not, asking: "Why do kids stare at me?"

Mom
: between.

Son
: between.

Sans camo.

A comfort with each other
: odd freedom.

–7–

A year prior to London. It's her cousin who tells her the story.
Farm fields unfurled. Her cousin's mom arriving one day.
Unexpected.

Oscar. Left alone.
Strips of wallpaper piled up in her crib (pulling at what's beneath).

Her aunt gets a glimpse.

Fifty-nine years later. Upon hearing this story. Oscar gets a
glimpse too.

To foil: run over or cross (ground or scent) to confuse the hounds.
How it's done. Oscar. Never taught. Not her instinct. But her
mother adept at.

Oscar outside the pack(t).

–8–

Narrow sidewalks of London. Everyone jockeying. Close shaves
of near collisions. Each step: assessment/decision. This way? Or,
that? Shoulder checking before stopping. Or turning. No A to B
assumptions. No stay to this side. A world of difference in motion.
Mostly wordless. Occasional "Sorry." "Sorry." Or, unnerving racial
flare-ups.

Oscar searching for Virginia and Leonard's house. Making way to Gordon Square.

There. Green exhale.

Small chestnut spaniel — perky tail — skimming grass soundlessly — like light on water.

Oscar spots empty bench. Purple beech canopies. A tree Virginia likely knew.

Green exhale — spaniel skimming.

Virginia's "when the pen gets on the scent" (Oscar's compass).

Oscar opens notebook.

Resides.

– 9 –

"Narrative and The Lie." Oscar's essay. Three-quarters finished. Intended to work on it while in London. Has not. Needs to turn away from pandemic prevalence of. Also, question of publishing. Who would?

Narratives that provoke resistance.

To being read. At all.

Oscar wishes otherwise. Yet these are the narratives that seek her out.

Readers' resistance: how to take into account?

For writer has them too.

1914. Camo and cubism. British military needing to get an edge on. Two of its officers/artists invent "disruptive pattern." Cubism inspiration for.

Announcement of war paint, agreed upon duel at dawn, eye-catching uniforms morph into first "war of deception." Camouflage.

A different mindset.

Utterly.

Tate Modern. Unexpected encounter with another Oscar's words:

"The final revelation is that lying, the telling of beautiful untrue things, is the proper aim of art."

Where that Oscar's quest took him. On the battlefield of narrative. Outsider writing about insiders' lives. Evoking their posturing. With wit. Fondness. Entertaining them. While he lived his unacceptable life.

True?
Point of view with flare?

Then there's Oscar's body.

Being not either nor neither.

Not a fitting in.

Nor misfit flaunting out.

Even the most aberrant group garrisons its norms
: its not between.

– 13 –

Waterloo Station. South Bank, Lambeth. 30.03.07.

Oscar
: en route to Camouflage Exhibit.

Checks the station clock: 13.20. Decides
: I am Oscar.
Second proper name.

Seeking her out.

Betsy now also Oscar.

Began first few days in London: Oscar Wilde quote at the Tate;
the Oscar in Albee's play at Theatre Royal. Haymarket.

Began, actually, a few months prior. Former student's newborn
curled into her shoulder. Inquired about its name.
                                                    "Oscar."

Upon hearing
: surge of delight.

Albee's Oscar. Stranger elegant in his difference. Upon sight of. Introduced each time a startled Midwest character comes on stage. By Elizabeth — Oscar's unconventional companion — who appears to be utterly conventional, announcing (with Maggie Smith's wicked aplomb):

> "This is Oscar.
> Oscar is *Black*."

Every time. The audience's erupting laughter
: relief at each character's startled awkwardness (meaning, fear).

Camo's infiltration in today's fashion.

The aim?
Of camouflage?

To "see without being seen."

Voyeurism, counter-surveillance, deception, ambush.

Undercover fantasies played out?

Post bilateral mastectomy and treatments, others' expectations.
For prostheses. That Oscar.
> — pros(e)thesis —

Absurdity of
: bra-bind if you have them,
camouflage if you don't.

Not logical.
Logistical.

Her son's body-memory of head resting against Oscar's soft breasts. He signs: "You're a man." Confusion: missing anatomy compounded by Oscar's androgynous nature.

She signs, "No, I'm a woman." Puzzlement on his face.

Then, one day: "What happened?"

She makes the sign for "ill," then "doctor," then "scissors." Snips where each breast has been. Shrugs an "Oh well: I'm fine now" expression. Not wanting to alarm. Not wanting him to think it could happen to him: his visible anatomy. Him in the clutches of learning categorization.

Then. One day. He finds his way
: "You're my dad-mom."

Him now enough in the world. To name. Oscar's betweenness. For himself.

Part 2

Vancouver, Iowa 2007

– 1 –

Oscar. Divesting.

Odds of survival. Her body insisting upon.

        Oscar: disengaging from societal preoccupation
with.

Over which the bra still reigns.

Deftness of hand unlocking.

Insatiable greed for
: the spilling out.
Hands on.
Mouth acquiring.
Breasts enlisted.

The meaning of "Mine."

            Who has the upper hand?

– 2 –

Oscar of Between initially subtitled "A Story of Failures."

Several writer-friends recoiled, "No one will want to read it
with a title like that."

The longer she lives, the more interested Oscar becomes in
failure — what we consider it to be. How so often it's the
unnamed force that shapes story.

Cubism's dramatic escape from representational art.

Its quiet "borrowing" from African art.

First World War. The story tyrannizes us until it is understood.

Desperate realities made present in one painting; one sculpture.
Monovision made askew with different points of view.

Splitting on a scale never previously encountered. First World
War. Story tyrannizes us until it is understood. Splitting of
Adam's chest/rib into Eve. Splitting of atom/in the wings.

1907 = Cubism's first painting
: *Les Demoiselles d'Avignon*
/Picasso's angles on five female nudes/
(veneer of Venus stripped away).

Disruptive pattern on British warships
: 1914. A line crossed.

First World War
: first large-scale encounter with The Other.

Cubism
: first encounter with the other within,
and The Other shockingly close at hand.

Camouflage is an inherent strategy in much of the natural world, yet First World War's purposes were not really the same thing at all. Oscar returns to the *Camouflage* exhibit catalogue. Reads: "The transforming of a hunter's appearance had a spiritual dimension ... they believed they could acquire the speed, stealth or prowess of the animal they hunted." Yes. This emulation, as well as the use of masks and costumes in indigenous ceremonial rituals, sets ancient practices apart from contemporary warfare strategies of deception and their fashion-inspired spinoffs.

Camouflage "the art of survival." Humans ever at risk: no blending-in fur, feathers, scales. Human's "natural protection"? Outsmarting predators.

Oscar comes across snapshots of her in 4-H Club uniform. Shoulder-width sailor's collar, plain blue dress, men's tie-shaped white bow extending to arms, sensible white flats.

4-H for rural kids: Head, Heart, Hands, Health. "I pledge my head to clearer thinking ..." Thinking, however, in Oscar's case suspect.

The Better Grooming Contest. Difference between training and taking pleasure in. Submission. Oscar her mother's project. Sensation of paper doll's wardrobe tabs clamping down on her body. The judges — three other mothers. Prim with quiet scores. To settle.

Oscar standing. In church basement activities room. Feet together. Attempting polite conversation as if. Their hands alternately inspecting her. Ticking off ratings on form.

Hair (score?). Accessories (score?). Dress (score?). Nails (score?). Shoes (score?). Hose (score?). Girdle (score?). Slip (score?). Bra (score?). Underpants (score?).

What this felt like. The terms for this? There are none. Oscar winning second prize. Her mother's disappointment. Oscar's shame. Migrating into clamped-down anger. For tears alienate even more.

It is Oscar who can now write this story.

Part 3

Vancouver 2008

Category: Oscar's anathema.

Although others' descriptions of her loneness change over
the years — tomboy, headstrong, stubborn, independent, odd,
rebellious, arrogant, different, unrealistic — they all signal the
same condition: one who does not play enough by the rules.

Categories being embodiment.
Of rules.
Of self-regulating
: automatic surveillance system built in.

Oscar looks the word up in her dictionary.

Category:
"Any of the basic classifications into which all knowledge can
be placed."

An impossible — even perilous — notion.

The impulse of category far more about what is "not" than
what "is."

Then there. In the etymology:
"Greek kategoria, from kategorein, *to accuse*: kata – *against* +
agorein, *to speak publicly*, from agora, *assembly*."

... to accuse, speak publicly against from *assembly* ...

– 2 –

To weep.

Cry centuries

.

: the suffering caused by all this *against* and *accusing*.

– 3 –

— weep —

– 4 –

Every applicable category, every allocated label noosed Oscar.

In her sixtieth year, a new one surfaces in her mind.

— *person of between* —

And Oscar is at ease.

Resides.

– 5 –

Begins.

To notice a surprising array of

— other persons of between —

Then, their quiet recognition of

one   an/other.

Part 4

London, Devon 2008

– 1 –

Conflict inventor of categories?

Oscar watching B&W films about First World War and Second World War.

Struck by overlay of R&R on non-military, post–Second World War life. Prevalence of drinking, smoking, fast-paced shoulder to soldier repartee, women's eye-to-eye flirtatious fencing with men and ease with calling the shots.

Oscar born on the heels of, yet the shoe fits her like no other.

– 2 –

The way Oscar occupies public space instinctively: her directness of gesture and speech. Repercussions of on a practical level.

– 3 –

Oscar of between. Between. Eras. Errors.

– 4 –

Time is everything with everything.

The difference between: The First Time; The Last Time. And between? "Time will tell."

Virginia journalling about her nascent sense of writing *Mrs. Dalloway*, how the "life of a woman" … might be told with almost "one incident — say the fall of [a?] flower … my theory being that the actual event practically does not exist — nor time either."

Stein writing narratives outside of time.

Einstein's world-shattering relativity.

Cubist conflation of times/place.

Time as the DNA of all interacting elements — apparent & not — at any given time?

– 5 –

Oscar back in London eleven months later. How one picks up where one left off — as if. Almost as though there had been no gap in. Time. Almost as though it had been a few days since she saw Shaun. Saradha. Though much has transpired much now becomes unstuck from linear time. Bits of much surfacing unpredictably here & there in response to this here, here. And now. A series of convergences and reconfiguring that makes Oscar giddy: narrative briefly on the loose.

Oscar having just dropped her beret amidst rushing feet while standing in vain effort "out of the way" searching for notebook in which she wrote down which platform to meet Shaun on but one does not stop in London, nor stand still, one moves, quickly, sits only rarely when one can snag a seat. Since her arrival two days ago Oscar clumsy not so much jet lag as different bodies in different space each place having its own kind of fluency. Vancouver stride all angle & awkward here amidst Londoners' rushing sidestep. Then her name is called out: it's Shaun. And Thomas. Hugs. Then off to fetch food for the train at Marks and Sparks outlet; then Saradha at Arrivals & Departures Board. Hugs. A force field gathering among them. Shaun's name called out — it's Pascal on his way to their retreat: introductions. Then Saradha notices

"On Time" suddenly changes to "Cancelled." Consternation. "What?" Speculations. Then the announcement: "We apologize for any inconvenience ... due to a fatality on the tracks ... all trains arriving and departing Paddington Station are cancelled for two to three hours." The five of them casting about; considering options while Shaun is on his mobile notifying retreat staff, students on way to meet them in Exeter, taxi booked to drive them from Exeter to Totliegh Barton. Londoners familiar with transit closures, breakdown, cancellations. They decide: tube to Waterloo Station for train to Reading; transfer there. Just make it. In time. Stops at every; after first two stops Shaun gets off train feeling ill – somehow will find a taxi to take him to Reading. Underlying sensation of mass fleeing. At Reading: no Shaun. Platforms rapidly filling up; no train to Exeter on Arrivals & Departures Board. Then announcement: "We apologize for any inconvenience caused in your trip but due to a fatality ... " no, not the same but another — this time on the line between Leeds and London. Thin tissue of civility damming mounting panic. Odd intimacy between these two suicides set in motion with us hundreds of thousands distressed commuters stopped in our tracks. These two they will never know any detail about other than the impact of their despair. Thomas comments they can determine difference between jump and push: those pushed arc farther over the track; those that jump land square in the middle. Saradha saying "February is suicide month." Shaun arrives! Oscar finds a spot for him to sit and gives him reiki: "Is it helping?" "Yeah, it's comforting." The announcement "apologize for any inconvenience ... due to a fatality ... " repeats every few minutes intensifying anxiety. Then Saradha sees a train to Exeter has just been posted; they scramble to the platform. It immediately fills to brim. Shaun and Oscar finding a spot standing in front of luggage shelves, constantly subjected to a stream of people squeezing by their backsides as they board and exit, gradually noting how passengers select different parts of their bodies to rub against as they pass by. Others are crammed into the exiting and entering end of our train car. A camaraderie soon erupting among the clutch jammed in there who make light of. Hilarity crescendos in the face of near chaos. Antidote to collective panic. Skill developed in & between air raids generationally passed down. Oscar buoyed by this resiliency yet aching for the two dead; sobered too by our rampant reliance on efficiency — how it makes us so helpless — how a few moments bring us to near brink of collective collapse.

–6–

Night before. Oscar staying with Myrna, Canadian writer friend who's flat-sitting in Islington. Talking writer talk. Oscar acknowledging her longing for a stretch of writing time. This kind of time having been a very long time ago. Myrna puzzled why Oscar hasn't had it. Then the delicate discussion of money and writing grants. Myrna's "Why?" Oscar's reply: "I can't get a grant." Myrna's "Why?" Oscar's shame about being repeatedly turned down; about even mentioning this. The symbiotic relationship between shame and blame. Categorization part of the problem. Must only tick one genre box on application. Oscar's writing rarely in one box — thus Oscar boxed in.

Myrna: "Which box did you check?"

Oscar: "Creative nonfiction." Them both creative nonfiction writers albeit of different stripes, Oscar takes the risk and gives Myrna the section of *Oscar of Between* submitted with application. This waiting like no other waiting when someone is reading your work.

Upon finishing, Myrna says: "It's not creative nonfiction."

That sinking feeling. "Why?"

"It's not discursive. Creative nonfiction is discursive. It's poetry."

"It's not poetry. No poet on a jury would consider it to be poetry."

Then they debate memoir. Oscar maintaining memoir isn't discursive but can be creative nonfiction. Yet she herself not convinced *Oscar of Between* is memoir.

"It's about perception — how perception happens, or doesn't happen, individually and collectively."

"You're writing something new here."

"How long is new new?" Then thinking *maybe it is memoir:* a memoir of ideas.

What to do when there is no category? The subterranean connection between category and camouflage, without category understanding askew, even improbable
: no box, no camo, no cigar.

They concur: an additional genre box is needed.

Myrna says "Mixed-genre." (mutt?)

Oscar "Cross-genre." (hybrid?)

– 7 –

Oscar. Thomas. Teaching Chroma Writing Residential. Their writers' workshops huddled at Arvon Foundation amidst bird-song-strung air, sheep-clouds just perceptibly in motion, pheasant-strut on intense green of cresting hills. Writers from many corners of, utterly disparate, desperate for context that will embrace them. Writers who are queer. Rare territory they have found during their four-day workshop soon to disintegrate. How to stay in touch?

In her closing words, Oscar rises.
Spontaneously holds up a blank sheet of paper.

"This is my homeland.
This is our homeland."

Part 5

Vancouver, Devon, Iowa, Mexico 2008

– 1 –

A grey and drizzle Vancouver 2008 Sunday. Oscar unable to
focus. A week ago. Flew her son back. To his other mother's
home. Damp and dank of sadness — Oscar closed in by it —
while simultaneously closed out of intimacy with her son.

Circling writing. Dog instinctively beating down grass, its pre-
domesticated memory intact despite laminate floor chill.

Sadness — disenchantment with words then camouflaged with
other words?

Oscar recalling her lines from *What Holds Us Here*
"and whether story entertains, claims, blames or explains its
instinct the same:
                    to keep sadness at bay"

– 2 –

Oscar
: grey on grey.

– 3 –

London and Devon. The dwellings Oscar stayed in built in
the seventeenth, sixteenth and eleventh centuries. Everything
infused with craftsman skills, bodies, time contrasted to
machines, chips.

Upon returning, Vancouver's buildings seem flimsy in contrast.
When Oscar mentions this, her Turkish friend Alev replies:
"Yes! So noncommittal."

The impact. Implications of.

– 4 –

Oscar. Between. At ease with a wide variety of people yet feels a despair too for loyalty is then uncertain. Oscar, close to many yet a loner. Never adept at simulating those she was born into. Knew. At a young age. That. She would have to. Leave.

Would ride her horse down to the river two miles away. Sit on her favourite rock. Whisper: "The river goes somewhere where people are more like me."

Who those people were? She didn't have a clue.

– 5 –

Spiegelman's graphic novel *Maus*. Its encounter with public versus private authorized narratives. Spiegelman, pulling Holocaust stories out of his belligerent, reluctant father. Oscar, plucking out stitching of stories sewn silent over decades.

– 6 –

Spiegelman "influenced by cubism."
Cubism's compilation of inevitable complexities and ambivalent complicities.
Time + angle = perspective, collapsing linear time, mindsets and events to disclose virile relationships previously denied = unrecognized.

April, 2008. Last month in Mexico: collision of times. Oscar
still recovering from. Holiday with two high school friends
Oscar had not communicated with for decades. They, having
kept in touch, tracked her down on the Internet, urged her
to join them. Trepidation. Oscar's life so off the map. Aspects,
timing of, often incomprehensible even to those close to her.

Oscar sitting at the breakfast table with her two high school
friends — Margaret asking her what she is working on now
— Oscar quickly sketching out *Oscar of Between*; her urgency
to find a term for herself that fits, invents one for herself: "a
person of between." Margaret's curiosity pricked. She asks
Oscar to define the term. Margaret, a non-Mexican Mexican,
anchored her entire adult life there. Oscar describing how
persons of between can appear on the surface to have little or
nothing in common yet once they understand betweenness,
suddenly recognize one another.

Margaret, not one to expose her interiority, quietly comments:

"*That's* interesting."

Part 6

Iowa, Vancouver, Windsor 2008

Iowa. The Des Moines River. River of Oscar's youth. In the middle of the river, these large white block letters repainted on the big rock by some mysterious person every summer.

JESUS SAVES

It became the farming community's way of measuring accumulation of precipitation:

"The river's above **JESUS SAVES** this morning!"

2008. Floods now of Biblical proportions in Iowa. Scorching temperatures in Toronto. Vancouver's "June-uary" the coldest in fifty-three years. Nature turning its back on our calculated bottom line.

– 2 –

Vancouver. A Writers' Studio event. Elee asks: "How was your trip to London? Did you do any writing?" What to say — Oscar quickly assesses — decides to take a risk. Abridges: *Time Out* "Museums" listing jumping out at her; sense of a nascent narrative circling her; immediate revelation upon entering camouflage exhibit; lifelong inexplicable bewilderment exiting her body. Oscar notices Elee's deep attention; softening of body; paling as though something is reorienting within her; then flush of face as Elee responds. "That's amazing. I really felt that." Then. Their mutual recovery. Oscar quietly stunned.

– 3 –

Camouflage: "the art of survival." Not born into it. No fur no shell nor feathers nor scales to protect from predators. Must be taught. Oscar and her mother: failure to imprint.

– 4 –

Vancouver. Fall of 2008. After fourteen years of a long string of
rentals and sublets, Oscar has a home again — a small condo
apartment with private patio on Charles Street.

As she stands at the sink, doing the dishes, Oscar wonders
about it, yet again. How is it that she was never taught the basic
survival skill of camouflage? Then, a surge through her body:
might her mother have unconsciously believed Oscar would be
safer without it? Thwart abuse (sans female camo)?

– 5 –

Just what is the difference between camouflage and an imposter?

– 6 –

2013. Charles Street, Vancouver. Oscar selecting and revising
excerpts for posting on upcoming July Oscar's Salon. Noting,
now, that she never responded to this question she posed to
herself five years ago. Oscar goes to dictionary given to her by
her parents in 1982. Re-reads her mother's inscription: "We
hope this will be helpful in your future writings." Writings
(and subsequent books) that Oscar never mentioned to her
parents; nor did they ever inquire after Oscar gave them a copy
of *A Gathering Instinct*. Her first book. Oscar's brother visited
shortly after and was privy to their mother's plan to take a
razor blade. To. Oscar's book. Cut. Out. The first twenty pages.
Pages about the demise of Oscar's marriage. Before. Before her
mother would show the book to her sisters. On the strict. Strict
condition that they never. Never. Never mention it to their
husbands. Nor, for that matter, anyone.

It becomes clearer. Clearer, as Oscar considers the etymologies and definitions of camouflage and imposter.

Camouflage, *camoufler*, to disguise from, *camouflet* ... smoke blown into one's nose, hence "disguise" ... "hot face" ... 1) ... concealing people or things from the enemy, 2) ... conceal by altering the appearance ...

Imposter, *imponere*, to put on ... A person who deceives under an assumed identity ...

Camouflage as a strategy and signalling of membership — even a duck hunter alone still uses the same camo gear, blinds, decoys that other duck hunters use.

Camouflage = collective and sanctioned.

Whereas, an imposter not only puts on (here's the rub) but assumes another's identity.

Imposter = individual and unauthorized. In the absence of being camouflaged, is the underlying suspicion then that you're an imposter?

Oscar " ... not really a ... "
Not really a normal girl nor suitable daughter not a welcomed member of the literary community not a proper wife nor without question woman, not a normal employee nor a real mother, not a loyal American nor true-born Canadian, not a conventional administrator nor an easily qualified pay-cheque mortgagee, not a lesbian writer widely read by lesbians, nor housed in an acceptable body, not a _____

: membership questioned at every turn.

Glare, stare, panicked admonishment:

> "You're in the *wrong* washroom!"

− 9 −

Oscar about to go out the door to the hospice. Give her dear
friend Diana reiki.

— the preciousness of this time together —

When they finish, Diana's boney hand ever so gently cups
Oscar's left cheek and they tenderly look in one another's eyes.
Oscar leaving to work in Ontario for a week.

− 10 −

2008. Fourteen storeys high in the Hilton. Looking down
on the Niagara River, Windsor Ontario side. Oscar there
launching *Silences*. A book Oscar edited. Thirty-six academics
writing on. The river surprisingly beautiful. Changing colours
constantly with cloud shadow; coming & going of light. Boats
of all sizes plying it periodically at variable speeds; at various
tasks. River a horizon.

In 1963, at sixteen years of age, Oscar made her first visit
here, on the Detroit side of the river. The Luther League
Convention. A group from her church taking the train to
attend. Detroit. Their anxious mothers. Sewed them all
matching plaid jackets. Membership flags of their little rural
community worn on their torsos. Oscar now gazes across at
Cobo Hall: site of their convention. Recalls. Viscerally. Keynote
speech by Black anti-racist activist on how ingrained racism

is in the English language: "little white lies" contrasted to "a black lie;" "Angel Food Cake" contrasted to "Devil's Food Cake." A long list. Oscar elated by his intelligence; integrity. His exposure of English's unacknowledged biases.

Language could encounter silences.

It was then she became a writer.

– 11 –

2001. Two weeks after 9/11. Windsor, Ontario.

Conference on Canadian Modernist Women Poets organized by Barbara and Di. Oscar, giving a reading from *Only This Blue* and a paper on Phyllis Webb's decision to stop writing and shift her creative inquiry to painting.

Rampant panic. AtmosFear of. A plane's normal descent of "controlled fall" taken out of control.

To get on a plane suddenly a life & death decision.
Then arriving: being that close to *it* (the US "under attack").

— the wide Niagara River suddenly a perilously thin line —

Use "extreme caution." An impossible imperative. How to recognize a terrorist? And, then what?

Presenters agonizing. Then, cancelling.

More attending (majority within driving distance).

The stronger instinct — to gather in the face of it all.

2008. While on the fourteenth floor, Oscar watches a documentary on the Florentine painter Paolo Uccello. Uccello utterly obsessed with three-dimensional perspective, constructed his paintings on a sketched-in underlying "ghost field." Perspective map for each painting. His "Battle of San Romano" (ca. 1456) to become the organizational template for commissioned British First World War artists; the figurative template for Picasso's *Guernica* (1937).

By almost five hundred years, Uccello's ghost field foreshadows Cubism.

Camouflage waiting in First World War's wings.

Second World War: the "Ghost Army." The US secretly invents a pretend advancing regiment to convince the Nazis there are no gaps in the Front Line.

As Oscar gazed through her fourteenth-floor window, the story of who we are in cubist relationship to other selves and our shared ghost fields came into focus while Diana began quietly evacuating her stories 3,000 miles away.

Vancouver. Five days and nights now. Began when Oscar returned. Diana's body beginning to signal its final hours: cooling of extremities, mottling, changing of breathing and pulse, hints of bluing hands and feet.

Beginning. Then reversing. Then beginning again. Reversing. An inching in and out. In. Out. "Anytime" becoming "no telling." Testing the water yet something yet to transpire? In herself? In one or more of us surrounding her? A waiting. Not a resisting. The startling "H" veins on either forehand flashing between thumb and index fingers. Thumb: will. Index: direction. The way we write a word in blue ink on our hand to remember. Something. Horizon not a demarcation but confluence? Of everything? Everything in. And out? Of light and dark without impediment. Without the punishing line of our judgements?

– 14 –

Oscar. Gazing through her fourteenth floor window. The story of this trip; who she is now in cubist relationship to other selves.

While Diana quietly evacuates her stories 3,000 miles away.

Part 7

Vancouver 2008

Oscar hunches over writing pad, mind jabbing back fear
to write this. This *this*, that is of little interest to those who
insist this *this* does not exist. The literary seen. For decades
Oscar within but not: a knot cinched tight. Her own growing
complicity. Recently removing some evidence of this *this*
when preparing her second round of literary archives; speaking
less and less to her writing friends about being ostracized,
understanding their need to stay on the right side of the right
people, understanding the greater the force of denial the
greater the fear of losing personal power.

To not stop. Stop. Writing.

Over the years, Oscar has considered it numerous times.

Some of this knot has been Oscar's doing. Lesbianism and
feminism infused her books from the beginning.

Some of the knot has been a state of affairs (private and public)
far more complex than anyone will acknowledge.

In 1984 (here another *Nineteen Eighty-Four* springs to mind),
Daphne and Oscar crossed a taboo line with their books of
erotic love poems.

— deep tremors of response —

No two women writers in English Canada had ever done
this before.

Nor have any two women since.

This was, is, male. Subject. Matter.

A line was crossed. But crossed with a difference between them. Daphne, a well-established author, had fourteen books. Oscar was an interloper with only two.

– 3 –

Now when teaching emerging writers, Oscar cautions, "Be careful. Although we often refer to ourselves as a 'tribe,' the literary community has almost nothing in common with an indigenous tribe. Status, professional alliances and likeminded friendships define us far more accurately."

On The Drive, Oscar waits to meet a friend for a coffee date at The Continental. Says hello to two writers across the room of the literary knot she wrote about just an hour ago. One is texting; the other reading. She respects them, even senses their own underlying vulnerabilities, yet knows one has caused her professional harm.

Oscar writes this as she waits.

She has. Not. Stopped.

– 4 –

During the 1980s then '90s, Oscar fell in love with two literary men's partners. Although the falling in love was mutual, Oscar was blamed. Since then, Oscar's observed, literary men are not ostracized for becoming lovers with literary men's partners.

There. Lies. The just. Of just-us.

In a 2013 *Margento* essay for the first time Oscar wrote:

"In hindsight, I realized that I emerged as a feminist lesbian author and this was an aberration. Other feminist lesbian writers' lives hadn't unfolded this way. In their early publishing years they had had close friendships with, a number had had romantic relationships with, and nearly all had been students of literary men. I had not. Consequently, my inclusion in the poetry community was significantly limited."

– 6 –

In early morning reverse twilight crows caw overhead Oscar's winging back from their nightly roost in Burnaby. Their daily to and fro comforting as the opening and closing of a book. They're said to number 16,000. Safety in numbers.

Part 8

Vancouver 2008

In her 610-square-foot nest Oscar perched on axis of
Vancouver's soundscape. Sound belonging. Hearing the first
sense to develop; last to leave as we die. Bearings. How sounds
wrap themselves around us, tide in and out, stroke our forehead
in our sleep. The city's echolocation: sending out sounds to
know where it is; who it is among. The hear of here. The sky
of wheeling seagull calls, freight train whistle caress of night-
valley's contours, descending two-note foghorn resonating in
our bones, proclamation of old Hydro Building's noontime
blare, whine of heron-like cranes loading ships, rattling-full
dumpster diver's shopping cart down alley, seaplanes' groan-
buzz into flight, evening cruise ships' silky horn of privilege,
dog's high-pitched howl at approaching siren, eagle's staccato
notes overhead, muffled firing of Stanley Park's nine o'clock
gun, murder of Burnaby-Vancouver-Burnaby crows' cawing
in dawn/cawing out day overhead, Oscar in the midst of it all,
made sound.

October. Vancouver. 2008. Sunlight through millions of new
planes of colour that reflect off colour fallen on ground. To be
cupped: held between the palms of these shimmering hues.
Oscar rushes outside every moment she can.

The Vancouver International Writers Festival: Hal Wake
interviewing Sharon Olds to a sold-out audience. Olds
acknowledging her twenty-five-year refusal to agree that her
poetry was "merely personal." Her corrective? Twenty-five
years of insisting it was only "apparently personal."

(all those years = the necessity of)

Then, Olds recounts, after using her routine disclaimer with a
young woman interviewer recently, noticed something.

Noticed. The young woman's face collapsed into a silent sadness.

Noticed. The toll.

Disarmed. Now secure, Olds decides it's time to "abandon it" — relinquish her camouflage.

Part 9

Saskatoon 2008

Saskatoon. October 2008. Oscar becomes Charlie on
Halloween. At her son's request. He is dressing up as Chaplin
and wants her to too. This surprises Oscar but she agrees. At the
school Halloween party, then the next night trick-or-treating,
some respond to Charlie Senior and Charlie Junior with
delight. Most do not. Only focus on Junior. More say nothing
at all. Are uneasy. Coolly stare.

Sr. and Jr. enjoying themselves despite the conundrum.

–2–

Three weeks later Oscar considers Charlie Sr.'s & Charlie Jr.'s
connotations. What was her son's longing? For a brother? A
dad? Or simply someone else who was the same as him for a
change? One thing is clear: for the first time, they shared the
same markings. Signalled family. Undeniably.

–3–

The difference between costume and camouflage? Oscar's
son was in costume, but Oscar? Oscar now thinking she was
in camouflage. Not intentionally but at the invitation of.
Disruption of others' expectations. Charlie Sr.'s gender not
automatically evident. Vexation. Who, exactly, was pulling what
over whom?

–4–

Much later,
Oscar considers another possibility: suspicion.
Suspicion that Oscar was. An. Imposter.

Part 10

Vancouver 2009

Oscar sipping morning green tea. Crow catches corner of
Oscar's eye with a sidelong glance as it sidles atop neighbour's
fence in nonchalant nervousness; flies few feet to hydrangea
(sidelong glance again). Oscar notices something in its beak
which crow deftly inserts into snow; plucks hydrangea leaf from
above; taps leaf down on its prize; final glance, then lifts off.
Moments later another crow lands on fence above hydrangea.
Struts. Assesses. Appears to pick up the scent of prized morsel.
Swoops down to ground around hydrangea as first crow returns
to fence feigning naïveté. Disinterest. The other walking that
rocking crow walk does not spot it. Turns. Calls back to the
first as it flies away.

The other follows. Time will pass. It will return later on its
own.

Camouflage has clinched its plan.

A few mornings prior, Oscar hears Tom Allen's account on
CBC of recent study in which a young baboon was chased
by its irate mother for some wrongdoing. As the mother
baboon nears her young offender, it unexpectedly halts, points
accusingly at another. Screams in alarm. All eyes divert as the
young trickster handily escapes.

The researcher's conclusion?

The greater our intelligence, the more we deceive.

Our perfection of lying possibly our paramount achievement.

–4–

Recent research discovery: the brain of the crow is far more similar to the monkey's than to the brains of other birds.

–5–

Concealment. Or camouflage.
(to?) lie in waiting (for?)
Lie (always) in waiting.

In her unfinished essay, "Narrative and The Lie," Oscar wrote: "There is never 'a' lie but immediately a second lie — the one we tell ourselves that we've not told a lie."

Part 11

Vancouver, Iowa, Germany 2009, 2012

2009. For over a year now in her new apartment, Oscar awakened by sounds of explosions overhead. Gunfire. Off and on. Day and night. Penetrated by. Sometimes she puts in earplugs (as she has just now). Sometimes, she puts on a CD to camouflage the violent sounds. And sometimes, she puts her fists to the ceiling. Pounds until the old logger turns down his television.

Oscar unnerved.

The more vicious the violence, the more we want it.
In our homes.

To help us while away the hours.

Relax.

– 2 –

Before.

Oscar. Nine years old — riffling through old *LIFE* magazines — sees photos of prisoners of Bergen-Belsen, the first concentration camp to be liberated by the Allied Forces.

These photos her first exposure to unbridled violence

— survivors'///////eyes —

look at camera in a way Oscar has never seen.

Before.

She can't take her eyes off their eyes so beyond expectation of ever being seen
as humans again.

After.

These eyes haunt her.

– 3 –

Years later, Oscar searched for this photo on the digital archive of *LIFE* magazine. Vacant eyes behind barbed wire not in there. Extended her search. Found a similar photo, "The Living Dead of Buchenwald," taken on April 16, 1945, by Margaret Bourke-White.

Bourke-White not first.

George Rodger was the first photographer inside Bergen-Belsen, April 15, 1945. His photographs, published in *LIFE* a few weeks later, are "highly influential in showing the reality of the death camps."

After.

He quit. Caught himself out, how he'd looked for "graphically pleasing compositions of the piles of bodies" amidst the trees, helter-skelter in deep burial trenches, throughout the buildings.

Never worked as a war correspondent again.

– 4 –

In 2012, Oscar is riveted when she reads *A Woman in Berlin* by Anonymous — yes, " … was a woman" — its unflinching account of the rape of 100,000 women and girls by the Red Army. Not published until 1959. The reactions from Germans confirm Anonymous's fears: the book is almost totally ignored or reviled for its "shameless immorality." In the 2002 reissued edition, the publisher writes " … German women were not supposed to talk about the reality of rape; and German men preferred not to be seen as impotent onlookers … "

Anonymous writes: "Our German calamity has a bitter taste — of repulsion, sickness, insanity, unlike anything in history. The radio just broadcast another concentration camp report. The most horrific thing is the order and thrift: millions of human beings as fertilizer, mattress stuffing, soft soap, felt mats — "

Before.

Before Hitler's unbridled mass murder, he asked if any countries wanted to accept German Jews.

Canada's response?

"None is too many."

– 5 –

1982. Cornelia and Oscar biked on the Stanley Park Seawall in late summer twilight:

sensation of flying. Glint of smelts in narrow nets reeled in by solitary fisherman: impression of catching splits of moon. Oscar and Cornelia glide side by side on the curvilinear, darkening path. Then Cornelia began. Told Oscar about the U.S. television series "Holocaust," recently broadcast after strong opposition. Half the German population viewed it. On the heels of each episode, people poured into the streets. For the first time, talked. Openly. About. It.

Wept.
Lying low (appearances often lie).

Nazi Germany's elder generations finally exposed.

Holocaust revealed how un-storied this story had been to post-Second World War Germans. Shiver of recognition — Oscar penetrated — wondering if there is any greater violence than story-cide? Decades later, Oscar reading Lispector's *The Passion According to G.H.*:

> "'Give me your hand again, I still don't know how to console myself about truth.'
>
> But — sit here a moment with me — the greatest disbelief in the truth of humanization would be to think that truth would destroy humanization ... it [has] to be our great security ... "

Part 12

Montreal, Iowa, Vancouver 2009

– 1 –

March 2009. Oscar sipping her Emerald Silver Green morning tea, gazes at backyard tree's Matisse-like limbs against fresh blue.

Oscar. Waiting for Oscar. Having worked on writing the final essay for *Breathing the Page* all week. Oscar. Wondering, would Oscar appear here? Here being Montreal. In all this difference where she finds most affinity with other writers. Oscar sensing Oscar nearing for three days now — trying to elbow out more space.

Across adjacent backyard, "brassiere woman" torques down spiral staircase as Oscar tries to decipher her age. Yesterday, Oscar noted her methodic pinning of six halter-like brassieres on frigid clothesline. Oscar surprisingly prudish about display of private self. Yet, admiring nonchalant quotidian self assuming collective self. History. Others' rows of.

Oscar now recalling her mother's adamant instructions on where to hang underpants and brassieres. Without fail. Pin them up between bed sheets hung on adjacent lines. Prevent view of by occupants in passing cars.

In the Midwest, no flags of femininity ever raised.

– 2 –

When adult and urban, Oscar began to realize how transparent rural life was. The state of a farmer's fields, car, lawn, house, garden, his and his family's clothes, livestock all on display.

During family Sunday afternoon drives to "see how the fields are doing," her father's verbal and body language a platform for assessing other farmers' successes and shortcomings in management: proper living.

In the city, display becomes manipulation of impressions.
A businessman teetering on bankruptcy can still fool his
friends, the bank, even his family. Wear stylish clothes, drive an
impressive car, invent "junk stocks."

Camouflage the foundation for runaway credit.

– 3 –

Dinner with Verena. Talking about our writing projects. Verena
finishing manuscript of interviews with four elderly men and
women who left, or fled, Germany: eventually ended up in
Montreal. How three out of four of them only recently began
speaking German. All those decades of not. The shame, even
danger of it.

Ache of empty arms of language. To be held — again — in its
tender embrace.

Oscar speaks briefly of this manuscript: about betweenness; use
of one fictive device; impact of First World War invention of
camouflage — how it has infiltrated all aspects of public and
private life.

Verena, bewildered, asks: "How?"

Oscar cites governance, how US citizens abandoned their right
to be told the truth decades ago, settled for what only sounds
believable.

Verena, an aware woman, replies: "Oh … "

Later Oscar thinks — context. How it can no longer be
assumed; how this has become a pervasive problem in the
Western world; how she needed to establish the context
for her thinking more — should have cited corporate
marketing, how it is predicated on half-truths and lies.

Cited the tampering with images using Photoshop to suit. Cited the altering of our bodies with Botox, plastic surgery, make-overs, ever increasing array of anti-aging and cover-up products. Cited virtual relationships replacing actual ones. Cited how scientific and economic data about environmental breakdown, global market schemes, profitability of cancer are routinely manipulated, "massaged" into camouflaged jargon. Spins & pitches. Out-of-context stats.

The insatiable bottom line — dependent on this.

– 4 –

Unable to do it. Oscar just now hanging out her laundry. Stops. Stares. At the final items in the basket. Her underwear.

Rationalizes. They'll dry better inside. Wonders. Is this some kind of rare intimacy Oscar still shares with her mother? X-pose. Oscar's hanging out of her underwear is not the same as the other women on Plateau Mont-Royal.

Oscar's would be scrutinized.

Later, Oscar realizes that the gay guy who lives below has not been hanging his underwear on the clothesline either.

Membership not to be assumed.

– 5 –

Signals of membership often more subtle than obvious.

Café Rico yesterday, Erin talking about visiting her mother's village. One of her mom's final requests: "Spread my ashes there."

Erin talking of the Second World War Ukrainian Nationalists' strategy for figuring out who were the Ukrainian Poles. The person in question was asked the names of various foods. As simple as that: a word automatically emits from your mouth and your life is over.

– 6 –

Tea finished, Oscar perched at window watches sunlight a-shine on bare-limbed bushes and small trees making them look like rivulets, tributaries.

Grey cat jumps atop garden shed roof. Paws diagonally across — pauses midway to scan surrounds — then ballet-points down to crossbar of chain-link, highwiring it out of sight.

Oscar after tea still at window; grey cat across shed roof to chain-link fence intersect each morning at this time without fail. Grey cat reminding Oscar: allegiance to even our most banal of habits, fierce.

– 7 –

Gail and Oscar tucked in the far corner of Librairie Olivieri Bistro animated by food, wine, conversation. Gail talking of her time in New York, of her nearly finished novel, *The Obituary*. Oscar talking of her time in London a couple of years ago, when she began writing *Oscar of Between*.

Recognition of their related narrative preoccupations.

Gail's manuscript: surveillance.
Oscar's: camouflage.

At a rare reading by four feminist-lesbian/queer authors,
Oscar reads third. As is often the case, Oscar senses a gap in
the kind of listening her writing requires, a shift she can never
assume the audience will make. She thinks of the opera-loving
Venetians who called the space between stage and audience
"this gulf of sorrows." What if this audience refuses? Her throat
tightens as she walks up to read, excerpt from *Oscar of Between*
in her hand. Too late now, she has to surrender to it. A couple
of minutes into her reading she feels that particular silence in
the room of being at the mercy of the narrative. Then it's over.
Applause and an excruciating shyness. How to get from here to
there — her seat in the back?

Deep breath. As Oscar nears her seat his arm shoots out.

"Thank you!"
He shakes her hand vigorously.
"That was deep. I *like* deep."

In Oscar's daily life, when encountering someone, it goes
like this: some address her as a male; some address her as a
female; some begin with one and then switch (sometimes
apologetically) to the other; some identify Oscar as lesbian and
their faces harden, or, open into a momentary glance of arousal;
some know they don't know and openly scrutinize; some
decide female but stare perplexedly at her now-sans-breast-
chest; some are bemused by, drawn or relate to her androgyny;
and for some none of this matters.

Oscar's only desire — to be present to herself and them.

On days turbulent with unpredictable reactions, Oscar longs for simplicity of camouflage. Yet has no instinct for it. It would only put her at odds with who Oscar is.

Then she brightens. Oscar — person of between — notices another response from others of between.

Curiosity.

Part 13

Vancouver, Montreal 2009

– 1 –

Sunlight on sheet of writing paper reminiscent of Montreal but different. Here — being Vancouver — it is morning sun. There it was afternoon light through window overlooking rue Boyer. This light warm, diffuse. There it was more focused, even blaring through the glass. Here, Oscar thinking about memory and membership. Recalling Simon McBurney startling the audience at a Jewish Book Fair panel when asked how it felt to be back home in London again (having just flown in from Japan). Assumption: London his homeland; Tokyo is foreign. Simon candidly replying that in Japan, he is clearly an outsider and he felt more at ease but in the UK, he is an outsider who supposedly belongs.

Upon hearing — relief running through Oscar's body.

This said. Simply as fact. Publicly.

At the source.

– 2 –

First assessment in Montreal not gender but cultural: francophone or anglophone? Language the repository of memory: who is speaking to whom? This determining what is said, what is not, and what is meant: the how and why. In another country, to briefly be free of this responsibility with all its sharp edges; to briefly current along in the evident present like a child who leaves navigation of expectations and disparate histories up to the adults.

Oscar in Denis' apartment.

He in hers.

Not having ever met but sharing mutual friend. They discover delightful correspondences: both have stones placed throughout, similar Chinese teacups, same rectangle woven-grass baskets, bullclips on opened bags of food, and images here & there of spiritual figures — Christian for Denis; Buddhist for Oscar.

The art, books, the music they had anticipated; had spoken of on the phone, yet their apartments were utterly disparate home bodies. Unseen bodies they had agreed to occupy. Oscar. Finds it oddly comforting to submerge into Denis' memory-infused belongings that steadfastly remain untranslatable.

– 3 –

Oscar relearning the city, erratically stumbles upon memories of visiting there with Daphne, then, Susan. Les Entretien, Place des Arts, pathway on Mont-Royal quietly devastating.

– 4 –

Oscar in her sixty-second year. The list of deaths, divorces, dissociations lengthening. The dialogical nature of memory steadily eroding: shared recollection becoming solitary recollection. Accretion of this particular sorrow.

This, perhaps, the greatest grief —

This, perhaps.

– 5 –

What is the image for this? The metaphor for memory isolation? Where are the symbols in public representation? The statues? Memorials? Plaques?

A face surfaces in Oscar's mind.

A profoundly solitary face in a film.

Haunting close-up in Werner Herzog's *Where the Green Ants Dream*. Still gaze of elderly Aboriginal man in the Outback. Gaze utterly void of expectation, free of seeking reciprocity. This man, we learn, is the sole speaker of his tribe's language. Only one still alive.

Two decades later, his face still incised in Oscar's mind.

– 6 –

"Language is an argument against loss."

Anne Michaels. "In Conversation with Hal Wake." Last night at St. Andrew's-Wesley United Church. Burrard Street. Discussing her new novel, *The Winter Vault*. In response to a comment from the audience, Michaels affirms: Yes, there is "no unneeded word" in her writing. Every word deeply considered. This alertness evident in other questions. Oscar struck by her moral and artistic integrity. And a grief in Michaels that feels boundless.

The acceleration of loss. How pervasive it has become. Michaels noting that language is increasingly all we have left. The fact that fewer and fewer of us are buried where we grew up. So much left behind, taken from us, or destroyed.

Oscar resonating with Michaels yet also aware that language can also promote loss. Instill forgetting. Hijack veracity.

Michaels' unease with the production of replicas. A kind of erasure. Oscar thinking, yes: is often a form of camouflage.

– 7 –

Loss of shared memories. Why does she mourn them so? Is it because — as a solitary person — Oscar hasn't the distraction of building another repertoire with a new intimate?

Oscar sensing it's something about memory being a profound form of intimacy that remains loyal. Regardless.

Unbound by time in our recollecting mind, memory is not confined by time. Is impervious to our life changes. Even when we seem to forget.

Memory is not so much ours as we are its. We being merely a vehicle for it.

Its worker bees.

– 8 –

Oscar and a writing friend in the Vancouver Art Gallery café, talking writing and telling stories about their unfolding lives over lattes. Rainy Sunday afternoon. The city emptied out — calm — on Easter weekend, they talk about family memories and her friend's urgency to bring them into her manuscript (both parents having died recently). So many stories in need of rescue.

They speak in almost hushed tones.

Then image of Joan Didion's reaction to one of the interviewer's questions in a documentary Oscar saw in Montreal flashes in her mind.

"It must have been very difficult for you to write this book. What prompted you to write *The Year of Magical Thinking?*"

— high beams of Didion's eyes —

"No one had ever prepared me for what grief is."

– 9 –

Large shopping bag chockablock with produce slung over Oscar's shoulder, Oscar weaving through aisles at Granville Island Market heading for Italian pasta shop for last item on list when in crush-of-bodies Oscar's hand brushes against astonishing soft-warmth. Shock.

"What was *that?*"

Then, she recognizes it: hand of a small child at two o'clock in a back carrier.

Her son.

At that age.

Inside, Oscar crumples onto the floor while outwardly she takes a few more brisk steps to shelves and shelves of olive oil.

Part 14

Vancouver, Iowa 2009

Oscar. Divesting. Again. In 2006 it was 700 books to the
Saskatoon Public Library. One year later, it was giving, selling,
and donating 60 percent of her belongings from her rental near
Main on 22nd in order to fit into her little apartment. Two
years later, it's emptying out her self-storage unit on Wall Street.
Self-storage. Commonplace term unheard of a few decades
ago. When Oscar's self is no-longer-in-storage, she calls her
goddaughter Sophie. Will she give her a hand?

They walk down the long hallways to the erratic clanking
of Sophie pushing a dolly — soft groan of fans overhead.
The numbering logic for the units is confusing and the only
landmarks for identifying which hallways they've already been
down are rodent traps parked here & there. Their voices are
tentative as they try to locate Oscar's unit amidst the endless
ellipsis of doors padlocked against natural light, air, theft.
Mausoleum-feel. Everything permeated with dust. (… to dust.)
Then: there. Oscar unlocks her unit's door. At the sight of boxes
piled head-high she fights the urge to relock it. Walk away.

The relativity of meaning — how little or no meaning her
belongings have to anyone other than herself.

Decide. Decide. Oscar admonishes herself:
get rid of these things.

Some of it is easy (empty boxes saved "for the next move").
Some not: making the decision to throw away 400 of her own
books: *Inversions*, but mostly *Proper Deafinitions*.

Slicing open the top of each box, Oscar winces at their
gleaming expectant covers. She sets aside one box of each
book to take back to her apartment and wheels the rest out to
the dumpster. Throws them over its five-foot-high sides: thud.
Thud. Box after box. Oscar reviews her logic: tired of moving
them (thud) no market for them (thud), no room in her

apartment (thud, thud); can't afford the storage (thud). She does not change her mind.

A peculiar feeling — destroying books you have authored. Peculiar.

At least it's by her hand. Oscar thinks of Elizabeth Smart's irate parents buying up all Canadian copies of *By Grand Central Station I Sat Down and Wept* in order to burn them. Thinks of the Nazi bonfires of Jewish-authored books. Thinks of Jane Rule's wine barrels full of her first edition of *Desert of the Heart* and wonders what happened to them.

Tears. Press. Not so much for what she has destroyed (although this does appall her), but for the sheer generosity of books — how they give themselves to us to be written then entrust themselves to be held, read, in anyone's hands.

– 2 –

Then there's the gun. In its dusty, fake-alligator-hide case. She's been in a quandary about it for years. How to get rid of a gun? There's the practicality of the dilemma but also the emotional trigger it sets off. In the twelfth year of Oscar's life her Aunt Lyla advised Oscar's mother to send Oscar (perhaps a too-solitary girl of the farm and woods) to the YWCA summer camp. This is when she first encountered the fierce jockeying for popularity among girls — girls from cities and large towns who had attended the camp before and who came with friends. Within the first hour she does something she'd never even thought of before: she changes her name. Does it instinctively. Desperately. Had to become someone else. Becomes "Rusty." Since popularity wasn't an option maybe a surprising name might help. The other girls respond with at least some faint curiosity. After breakfast the first morning each girl must select a set of daily activities. A novice in all, Rusty chooses canoeing, water skiing, target shooting. She soon excels at skiing. At the end of the week, her canoeing group sets out on a two-day wilderness trip. Rusty is stunned by how the other twelve-year-olds set their alarm clocks a half hour early to meticulously apply their makeup before breakfast. Someone also steals her hard-soled moccasins.

Target shooting (another foreign activity) goes better. At the awards dinner she receives the Deadeye Dotty Award for the highest score for marksmanship.

That Christmas she had only one request: a .22 rifle. Her mother adamantly refused. "What would people think?" But on Christmas Eve, after all the presents were opened, her father said, "I think there's one more for you, Betsy, back under the tree." It was a long, narrow package. Could it possibly be? Oscar could barely contain her giddiness as she tore off the paper and pulled the gun out of the box. She glanced up: saw her father's smile.

He had seen her. As she was.

Now, as Oscar frets about what to do with the gun, she tells Sophie the story of the other controversial gift. For her seventh birthday, Sophie's only desire was for a Barbie doll. The very thought made her mom cringe, so Mary asked Oscar to do the deed. After her own recoil, Oscar recalled her father and the rifle. Her turn to bite the bullet, she bought the Barbie.

Sophie and Oscar decide to take a break after a few hours of sorting. Go back to Oscar's for a bite.

The rifle.

She cannot postpone this decision any longer. There's no one who wants it and her son has fortunately shown no interest in guns. While Oscar makes their lunch, she asks Sophie to call a few gun stores to see if one might buy it. A shop at 16th and Fraser is interested.

Upon returning, they finish loading the car with objects Oscar's moving back to her apartment. The gun is the final task.

Silently driving to the store, a peculiar kind of nervousness is circling around them. When they walk into the narrow shop their discomfort increases: it's teeming with customers. Some are the type of men you would anticipate; many are not. The mood is one of contained excitement. The conversations between staff and customers, and customers with other customers, are intensely focused. Sophie and Oscar barely speak, each as uncomfortable and out of place as the other. A young man next to them effortlessly spends $800. Oscar wonders, "What am I doing here?" and fights the urge to leave. Goes through the reasons again: it's worse to throw it away. Who might find it? Use if for what? Better to have it registered.

Odd how difficult it is to get rid of dangerous things.

The store buyer finally has time to wait on them. He takes the gun into the back room to inspect it and run a security check. Returns and offers Oscar $50. As he hands her the crisp red bill Oscar stalls inside herself with a small grief then recognizes that this story of two gifts suddenly makes sense.

Sophie is eagerly heading for the door.

Oscar calls out, "Sophie?"

Sophie turns around as Oscar catches up and hands her the crisp red $50. Sophie's face flushes with surprise.

"Why are you giving it to me?"

"It's yours. The rifle. The Barbie. This is how the story ends."

As Oscar prepares this excerpt for Oscar's Salon, she recalls another connection between rifle and Barbie. She does an online search to confirm it. It's true. The engineer Mattel hired to "re-think the design of a German doll called Bild Lilli" had previously designed missiles. Oscar finds an image of a 1993 Barbie, then an image of her .22 rifle's vintage. Rotates the .22's image so that the barrel points down.

Missile, Barbie and .22 share the same shape.

Part 15

Nanaimo, Hornby Island, Vancouver 2009

– 1 –

Mid-morn September clear-blue sky illuminates single line of
web strung over grass in every direction from hawkweed to old
stumps to fern to wild rose to salal criss-crossing, shimmering
everywhere.

Hornby Island, Deb and Drew's cottage. Oscar and Arleen
arrived yesterday. After unloading their cars, buying groceries at
the Co-op, Arleen and Oscar hike Little Tribune Bay. Feel their
way over sandstone and composite rocks whose shapes and
contours are so unlike shapes conceived by the human mind.

Arleen and Oscar talking as they climb about the era they
identify with: for Arleen, it's the '50s with its surge of the first
teenage-defined culture; for Oscar, it's the '40s with its self-
possessed, opinionated women who held their own.

In Nanaimo yesterday, Oscar searching for her bank to pay
Visa bill. The city maps and several residents' directions do not
coincide. The payment is due today. And, Oscar must drive
another hour to meet Arleen to catch the next ferry. Fifteen
minutes to spare. Residents of Nanaimo walk half speed on
the sidewalks. Oscar is in Vancouver stride mode. A retiree
gentleman exits a store and walks across sidewalk to his car.
Oscar swerves to right (near collision), then left. The man
quails. Stops in his tracks. Says, "I think I'll just stand still." Oscar
apologizes as she leaves him in her wake. Shame flits through
her: this is not how Oscar wants to move through the world.

– 2 –

The cottage's large back lawn is a courtyard of (yes, "towering")
cedars, firs, bigleaf maples, poplars, beech.

All night, Oscar hears them shushing the cold front pushing in
with their (yes, "countless") undulating layers of green.

Then, early morning cold rain scores air with its (yes, "thousands of") slanted dashes mirrored in her (yes, "entranced") eyes.

– 3 –

Deep night punctured by spotlight stars. In their conversation after dinner, Oscar confided in Arleen about how nearly all her writing companions were invited to a recent major feminist literary event except her. Then, how all Oscar's experimental feminist poet friends were included in a watershed anthology except her — this exclusion rendering Oscar's role in feminist experimental writing in Canada to be non-existent. Before, male writers ignored Oscar, then post-breakup, this became the modus operandi in the feminist literary community. At first she didn't believe it. Initially, when not invited to two major feminist literary conferences organized by friends, Oscar had contacted them. Both said they had "forgotten" to invite her, then did. But, the forgetting continued.

Last week Oana in town from Montreal. Over coffee, she raised the subject of the anthology, asked Oscar, "Why weren't you included?" Halt. No one. In sixteen years. Has raised the subject of Oscar's exclusion. Not one. Oscar takes a deep breath: Is there any benefit (to Oscar, to Oana, to anyone) to reply honestly? In the rare conversations with other friends before, Oscar met only with rationalizations and denial. Now, Oana genuinely troubled, is wondering, "Why?" Oscar respects Oana. Trusts her integrity. Decides to risk it. They talk briefly. Carefully. Oscar does not want to create awkwardness between them, nor for Oana with others.

– 4 –

Next eve after dinner, Arleen editing her manuscript. After working all day, Oscar is written out so is relaxing, stoking the fire, but Gurjinder's voice mail about a publisher conundrum presses. She tells Arleen she's going down to the point to access her cell phone server. Grassy Point. Azure-clean fall sky. Oscar reaches Gurjinder's voice mail, leaves message when she can call tomorrow. Turning to leave, Oscar notices an intense light low in the night sky over Texada Island. Venus? Seems too bright … watches it with growing unease for a couple of minutes then walks back to the car, inserts her key in the ignition. Looks up again. The light is far too big for a star. Oscar gets out of car. Plummets into all the possibilities of what this light might be. The light is stationary. Primitive panic rises in her. She attempts to dismiss it then notices the light is casting across the ocean with the brilliance of numerous moons.

Something is wrong.

Her mind scans all the eerie possibilities again. None fit. Then a jagged smoke trail begins to emit from the light's centre. Dazzling, disturbing, it hovers a few minutes, quickly sphincters shut, leaving a deep darkness.

It takes two days for Oscar to find someone on Hornby who saw it too. Who knows what it was:

"Military manoeuvres."

Part 16

Berkeley, Vancouver 2010

December, 2010, in a Berkeley sublet. Difficult to find her feet. Write. Extract herself from urgent work calls and emails, navigate racial and class tensions on the street. Reading Sarah Bakewell's *How to Live: Or a Life of Montaigne in One Question and Twenty Attempts at an Answer*. Montaigne the creator of the essay. Bakewell believes that the essay is "a form that melds the intellectual and the personal" and that to Montaigne, "The distinction between self-help and academic philosophy wouldn't have made much sense … he didn't bother accumulating facts … much more important was the exposure to someone else's experience and perspective." A connect. Oscar realizing she needs to read more of Montaigne. A connect last night also at the Chanticleer Concert when they sang "In the Bleak Mid-Winter" (tear rivulets down Oscar's face), the hymn Oscar sang to herself after her father died on Christmas Eve.

Her father. Montaigne. Oscar's dad had to quit school after grade eight to help on the farm but her father's intelligence and vision continued unabated on a personal and community-minded level. By watching him, she learned the inventiveness and insight gained with a mind not extensively schooled. Like him, observation is her lifelong teacher.

Oscar, in the U of C Berkeley library, reading J.V. Ramana Rao's definition of deception in *Introduction to Camouflage and Deception*.

"As applied to war, deception is a deliberate and rational effort to mislead the adversary by manipulation, distortion, or falsification of evidence to induce him to react in a manner prejudicial to his intent and/or to the benefit of the deceiver …"

He lists its "facets" as:

"Camouflage and concealment; deception equipment in the form of dummies, decoys, faints, and ruses; disinformation."

– 3 –

Last summer, Oscar finally refused to be complicit with the ruse. She contacted one of the editors of the anthology and asked her to elucidate exactly what the criteria for inclusion were. They emailed back and forth, had a phone conversation but the criteria were never elucidated. In Oscar's final email she wrote, "I am now willing to walk away ... perhaps you have done me a favour ... [for] it has become a community that does not support me, even erases me."

– 4 –

Early afternoon. Shaena and Oscar: the luxury of sitting in two armchairs in front of a fire. Shaena telling Oscar that she's beginning the novel all over again after her purse and notebooks were stolen out of her house while she was writing the first draft. Later, the thief kindly deposited the notebooks on her neighbour's garage roof. Shaena shows her one of the notebooks and Oscar is struck by the spatiality and textures of the longhand, sketches, images cut out, glued here and there. Oscar comments on how she's writing this manuscript in the form of entries as she did in *Bloodroot*. Recounts: her desire to write another creative nonfiction lyric prose narrative; instinct to introduce one simple fictive device; sudden magnetism of the name "Oscar"; compulsion to see camouflage exhibit where she understands an inexplicable force that shaped her whole life. Shaena says: "It sounds magical." Then, Oscar says things she's not said out loud before: that she's naming and has rarely used names in all her previous books. To name is a radical act for Oscar. Her "fictive" name has freed her to inscribe actual names of people, places, events, times — which in turn has enabled her to to tell her person-of-between stories.

Part 17

Montreal, Berkeley, Iowa 2011

604-681-1111. Yellow Taxi: "I'd like a cab for 9:30 at 1484 Charles Street, please." The dispatcher replies, "For Betsy?" (Oscar on their database.) "Yes." Despite the fact that Oscar is eager for her writing retreat she finds it hard to leave. Oscar could explain this to herself — it's finally summer in Vancouver, or it's intoxicatingly peaceful now that the construction is done — but it's simply that she loves her home; home her closest companion.

The phone rings: the cab's arrived. When the driver spots her coming, he jumps out and opens the trunk. "Good morning, sir." Oscar, who has long ago desisted in correcting people, carries on. "And a good morning to you!" As the driver pulls away, they comfortably debate various routes then agree on Great Northern Way.

[pause]

Oscar notes that his friendly mood has changed, that he keeps glancing up to the mirror with furrowed brow of uncertainty.

He turns on the radio. A man's voice sings unaccompanied.

"Morning prayers?" Oscar inquires.
He looks up in the mirror again and meets Oscar's gaze.
"Yes. In Punjabi."

After a few silent minutes they hit a bottleneck. He complains, "There's road repairs everywhere." Oscar retorts: "Yes, in the summer, road repairs and babies everywhere!" He laughs at this and they chat — discover that they both love babies — relax. The cab inching forward.

Sultry Montreal morn. The Plateau. Oscar in Denis' nest-level apartment. Vancouver: Denis in hers. Outside Denis' window the locust tree's eleven oval leaflets on either side of stem (with a solo one at each tip) shimmer like piano keys. Men's directive voices. Hammering. Clanking of scaffolding going up. Construction, construction: for two years on either side of Oscar's apartment and now here. Oscar turns her thoughts to her construction project: how to re-enter and build this manuscript after year-and-half absence. The finishing, proofing and promoting of *Breathing the Page* have gobbled up her already limited writing time. Oscar sighs. The "lance" of "free." Question of how not to fall upon its blade of never-say-no to work and other writers' needs that Oscar understands all too well.

The '60s popular sayings, "I need to take some space" and "Give me space!" Time inherent in space. Time + space = relationship. Oscar thinking how a change in any one of these initiates change in the other two. Within a few months Netflix wipes out three of the four video/DVD stores on The Drive, stores in which Oscar talked film with the staff. Gone. Time + space = relationship a-jumble.

Sight of a young woman walking while reading text message — flash of sensuous smile on her face — Oscar stumbling into her intimacy amidst a teeming sidewalk.

New iPad blanket ads in San Francisco's BART stations last December. Multiple posters of iPads propped up on users' laps and raised thighs, index fingers touching screens just above users' genitals. Only exception — African-American man — finger poised farther up the screen (racism still intact).

He boards the BART train midday at Oakland City Center. Stands tentatively just inside the sliding doors. Small man lost in layers and layers of clothing and too-large parka. To his immediate left, a young mother holds picture-perfect daughter on her lap. A few feet in front of him, Oscar and Ingrid sit. As soon as the doors close he begins in a quiet voice. "I'm so afraid. I don't know what to do. I'm afraid of me. And afraid what I might do to you ... " The mother (rigid with fear) stealthily moves her hands slowly up to cover daughter's ears. Oscar peripherally sees others' eyes are fixed on floor, windows, mobile devices. Only other African-American in the car — a well-dressed, handsome, professional man in his thirties with attaché case — stares straight ahead. Oscar takes the risk of letting him see she's listening. "I'm afraid of me. Afraid of you. I don't know what to do. I'm so afraid. I can't go on like this. I'm so afraid ... afraid what I might do to you." The train approaches the next station, slows (will he get off? take this train farther?). Halts. People gingerly walk around him to exit. Just before doors close he slips out. A perceptible sigh moves through the car. The mother's hands drop to hug her daughter. Conversations tentatively begin here & there. Oscar and Ingrid quietly comment on how profound his despair was — how he speaks for so very many — then fall back into silence.

"During the six years of my architectural education the subject of comfort was mentioned only once."
— Witold Rybczynski, *Home: A Short History of an Idea*

Upon arriving at Denis' in 2009, Oscar noted that despite the dissimilar architecture (space) and eras in which their buildings were constructed (time), Denis' and Oscar's sensibilities (relationship) to creating home were similar. Oscar puzzled over which man is Denis in the photos throughout his apartment, yet she felt immediately at home. Within days, Oscar wrote two of her favourite pieces: the final essay for *Breathing the Page*, "Sustaining Yourself as a Writer," and Part 12 of *Oscar of Between*.

Two years later, Oscar emailed Denis and asked if he would like to read Part 12 of *Oscar of Between*, which evoked a number of details about his apartment. Yes, he wants to read it. She sends it.

Several days later, Denis emails Oscar.

"I have read your Montreal manuscript just once, with great interest. Yes, the brassiere lady ... Rest assured: I never hang any underwear on the clothesline either ..."

– 6 –

2011. Iris of eye in her teal pajamas, Oscar awakens early each morn in Denis' white bedroom and white-sheeted bed. Gazes out tall window on her right. Watches how ivy on brick cups sunlight like an enchanted child's hands, its leaves move ever so slightly in a moisture-infused breeze after last night's storm. Oscar listens for the sound of the opening bars of Denis' neighbours' rising: pop of a balcony door opened; cupboard doors and drawers; flat and tableware jostled; *clink-clink-clink* of a spoon in cereal bowl; crescendo of kettle whistle then sharp chirp as it's lifted off burner; murmur of first exchange of words; recorder's lilt briefly played; staccato complaint of laundry line pulled after each item's pegging.

Difference between vertically entering the day and horizontally entering it — how Oscar cherishes it.

Arc of memory leaps to just over a year ago — the phone call — one of Oscar's students had died. Counselling had been arranged, Oscar had told her student she'd go to the next immigration lawyer appointment with her, pleaded with her, "Don't give up. Write about it — they can't take that away from you — don't give them that power." But the vortex was unrelenting. For days after the phone call, Oscar felt it in her body — the how — before police confirmed it. Her student had jumped. Jumped from her eighth floor balcony. No turning back.

This is where words turn their back on you.

Where space + time = relationship collapse.

Those weeks before, her student kept saying, "There's nothing anyone can do. Nobody can do anything."

Utterly alienated as an exile for twenty-five years in a European country, her brother executed in Iran, Canada was her only hope.

This is when denial of a visa translates into a death sentence.

Her student had been embraced as a writer but it wasn't enough. It was nowhere near enough.

This is where.

Words turned their back.

This is where we resort to a two-letter word: I can't take *it* anymore. I didn't see *it* coming. *It* will come back to haunt you. *It's* over.

This is *it*.

Side of Montreal brick building — 3 x 5 rectangle of grey paint obliterates graffiti. Post-cover-up, two words spray-painted on top of solid grey:

ART MISSING

In early morning thick heat thins.
A leaf parachutes down from maple.
With slight breeze, some leaves nod

                                oui

                       oui

                                    oui

while others wag back and forth

     non non/non non

Pintxos. Cuisine espagnole with Nicole last night. Each
pintxo an exquisite petit monde presented at a leisurely pace
as conversation stretched over three hours. Both compliment
one another on "how very good you look." Oscar, who enjoys
testing gros et petit theories with Nicole, now postulates that
Montrealers' lapsed Catholicism infuses their love of quotidian
ritual and sensibilities.

Doubtful, Nicole asks, "For example?"

Oscar cites the dominance of three-storey walk-up apartments on
the Plateau — how their architecture might reference the Trinity.

Startle on Nicole's face.

Then laughter as she shakes her head with recognition.

No new writing yesterday. Day of brutal heat, severe
weather warnings.

La canicule à Montréal.

Oscar, attempting to take a day off, succeeds until after lunch
when she finds herself negotiating with herself. "I'll do it for only
one hour." Starts keying in the opening pieces of this section.

Time, however, in all its articulated and unarticulated aspects, is
a different entity for writers. Whenever we attempt to relate to
it in a normal fashion we inevitably fail.

Oscar's one hour becomes seven.

That evening the neighbourhood eerily quiet except for
Mont-Royal where people perform necessary tasks as if in an
aquafit class while others seek refuge in every air-conditioned
café, bar or store.

On rue Boyer no one in sight. Balconies and backyards
empty. Sidewalks still. All move as little as possible.

With every exertion sticky-hot sweat floods skin and clothes.
To avoid increase in body heat — even lights not turned on
as darkness envelops. Oscar flees to her bed, naked. Fan posed
overhead on high. Imagines others doing the same.

A few hours into tossing & turning it happens without prelude:
muscular, pounding rain smothers heat, then

— sleep —

5:30 a.m. Oscar raises venetian blind to a sky she's never seen.

Shredded into layers and layers of small scudding fragments
are yesterday's bearing-down cumulus clouds. At the base of
each fragment remain heavy graphite smudges yet each cloud's
whimsical top and borders glow in the purest white Oscar has
ever seen.

Across softest of blues they move quickly as sixteenth notes.

"Drought: A Creeping Disaster."

In an article in the July 17, 2011, *New York Times*, Alex Prud'homme challenges the term *drought*, arguing that in many parts of the world it is aridification.

"In the South, 14 states are now baking in blast-furnace conditions … [and] wildfires."

Expanding aridification our most life-threatening phenomenon. Space (urgent need for conservation, regulation) + time (taxing usage, rainwater collection) = relationship (recycling, weather modification).

By 2025, the United Nations expects "global demand for water to increase by two-thirds."

How little we know water.
How deeply water knows us.

Our bodies 65 percent water. Our planet 70 percent water.

~ water's memory unfathomable ~

Macro to micro.
Detailed records of past climate and hydrology in every aquifer.
Soft-clear tears shed for current suffering; dense saline ones for suffering long held.

Eager to sit at the top of the spiral stairs — sip her tea in sun's caress — Oscar heads for the kitchen. Hears that the women next door are already smoking and talking on their balcony. On the fulcrum of post-Friday night and pre-Saturday night, Oscar notes how their conversation is animated with possibilities.

Never one for group feeding in the morning, Oscar heads down the hall. Eats cereal in sleepy shadows of front balcony. Back in kitchen to prepare tea, Oscar hears abrupt halt in conversation. Ahh! They have gone back inside. Carrying her tea down to the garden, she catches a glimpse — they're still there — oddly quiet. Snatching another glimpse she sees each is bent over something on the little table, transfixed. Reading books? Then Oscar sees reflected light on one's face. Oh, Oscar, you writing fool: not books. Mirrors! Each putting on makeup with such intensity it embarrasses her.

Oscar averts her eyes. Drinks tea awkwardly. Quickly returns to the front balcony for second cup.

Half an hour passes. Silence. Oscar decides to check it out. The two are still there. Utterly preoccupied as they make up for their deficiencies with a sense of plumaged hope.

On that fateful YWCA summer camp's canoe trip, when the other girls set their alarm clocks thirty minutes early to put on their makeup, Oscar realized there was no remedy. No viable camouflage. Girl? Boy? Oscar was not either/or. Not neither/nor, nor wishing to be.

Light-filled morn. Oscar walks down to Multimags to buy
Sunday edition of the *New York Times*. July 22, 2011, Norway: a
"Christian extremist" (camouflaging in a policeman's uniform)
gains easy access to a small island. Kills seventy-seven people.
All but two are youth at a summer camp for politically active
young adults.

Horror rises up in Oscar. The self-proclaimed Norwegian
hero of the war against multiculturalism, feminists and Muslim
immigrants posted a 1,500-page manifesto and video of himself
— in war camo with semi-automatic rifle — a couple of hours
before his attack.

This is it.

It's you or me.

One survivor, a Sri Lankan-born twenty-three-year-old who
moved to Norway at age three, is quoted as saying the camp
had been

"the safest place in the world."

Three years later. Twenty-two-year-old California student posts a lengthy manifesto detailing his hatred of women and racial minorities. Next night he posts a YouTube video before killing three Asian roommates — three women students — and wounding thirteen others. Then — surrounded by police — kills himself. His father a unit director of *The Hunger Games*.

Yesterday. Corner of Commercial Drive and Broadway — older Aboriginal man selling white T-shirt with black block letters:

ABORIGINAL HOLOCAUST:
1492-?

Part 18

Vancouver, Berlin, Montreal, Norway 2012

3 a.m. deep-sleep sound-sleep impact/shock glass-shatter-
scatters across floor. Oscar bolts upright — entire body
listens — entry? Shouting? Just back from Berlin. Artist's brass
cobblestones embedded in sidewalks here and there in front
of flats Jews pulled out of — name, birth date, abduction date,
camp name, extermination date inscribed — sudden intimacy
of those numbers those names that flat — taking you off guard.

Oscar up. Small flashlight in hand — circle of light searching
the floor — finds it. No note wrapped around brick but
another message. Glass splinters from framed poster for Writers
in Dialogue. A feminist literary event between Adrienne Rich
and Nicole Brossard that Oscar moderated. Toronto. 1981.
Five hundred people. Adrienne's recent death passing quietly
through the remnants of the feminist community. That brilliant,
nearly forgotten, long-broken era swept up in night.

Next day. Oscar strides asphalt sidewalk beside Britannia's
playing field. Pure blue overhead charms strangers into
exchanging smiles.

Then. There. Centre of sidewalk — gaping yellow beak —
no other remains just mandibles' arrested shock. Glimpse of
unnerving. Oscar dismisses (can't be) doesn't break stride. Then
stops dead in her tracks. Pivots quickly.

Yellow gaping mouth on black asphalt.

A scream alights in Oscar's mind.

Berlin. 2012. Oscar and Ingrid enter the walled cemetery. A short grey-haired woman appears in the lapidary doorway. Calls them over. Ingrid speaks French, Flemish, a little German. The caretaker speaks German. Oscar speaks none — watches in confusion, their confusion.

Usually prepared for it, this time Oscar is not. Then Ingrid gets it: "She thinks you're a man. You can't enter unless you wear a yarmulke."

Oscar notices the basket of skullcaps. "A yarmulke?"

"Yes."

Oscar's mind races — less trouble not to correct people (every customs officer has addressed her as "Sir" despite "Sex/Sexe: F" on her passport) — but here, she does not want to risk offence — what if the caretaker later realizes and feels she's been duped?

Body language: the urgent translation of.

Oscar enters the fray, says to Ingrid, "Can you tell her in German I'm a woman?" Then points to her chest and says several times: "I am a woman. I'm a woman."

The caretaker's face softens.
She waves them on.

Gaping yellow beak on black asphalt.
Jewish cemetery.
Brass letters on black marble stolen.
Pulled out like gold fillings.

Berlin. As with most old cities, the headstones are cheek by
jowl. Limbed, tall deciduous trees canopy black, polished
marble headstones with empty drill holes (like reverse braille)
where brass lettering once was. Re. Move. All. Oscar having
read that morning that the Nazis chiselled off names of
German Jewish soldiers on historical military monuments.

Here and there, vandalized headstones are a-tumble. Ivy covers
headstones and ground in various areas of the cemetery and
creates an eerie impression of figures sitting up in bed under
green blankets. Many plain stone markers so worn away by
"ravages of time" inscription eroded away.

No survivors are left to tend these graves.

As they walk toward the main gate to leave, Ingrid and Oscar
notice an agitated exchange between caretaker and a man
while his two women companions look on. Nearing their
clutch, Ingrid understands enough German to realize he's
refusing to wear a yarmulke.

Refusing, also, to leave. Insult; assault. Continues.

Outside the cemetery walls, Oscar's eyes are magnetized by an
English word spray-painted in three-foot-high white block
letters on building abutting wall of cemetery:

FREAKS

The yellow beak — diamond-shaped outline on black asphalt — a starling's. Its terror jarringly similar to its "feed me, feed me!" upon parents' arrival.

– 7 –

It was unbearable to look at.

– 8 –

It doesn't end there. It never ends there.

Since Oscar returned home, the dismemberment murder in Montreal. Videoed and posted on the Internet. Reported to the police. The police dismissed it as fake.

We don't want to believe it. Seldom believe it.

A severed hand mailed to an MP in Ottawa.
The torso found in a garbage bag on a Montreal sidewalk.
Week later: the other hand; foot. Mailed to Vancouver elementary schools.

Then,
a manhunt.

At an Internet café — the "person of interest" is recognized from an internationally circulated photo — police called. Is arrested.

In Berlin.

Vancouver. Home from Berlin, Oscar reads that Munch's *The Scream* sells for $120 million. As the gavel falls, it becomes the most expensive artwork sold at auction.

One of four versions, the $120 million version of *The Scream* is recognized as the best. Only this version has Munch's hand-painted poem written on the frame.

Montreal.
He was an immigrant student.
Gay.
His severed head (scream) still not found.
His parents want to return all his parts back to China.
Otherwise, he will not rest
peacefully.

The Berlin Secession, 1892.
" ... a group of artists removed themselves from the official Association of Berlin Artists ... after the association succumbed to pressure from Kaiser Wilhelm to shut down a show featuring Edvard Munch."
(scream)

In Munch's painting a male figure foregrounded on bridge — shattering sound emitting from his mouth.
(hands covering ears like parentheses)

– 12 –

June 3, 2012, the *New York Times*: "You're spending $120 million, in part, to show that you can blow $120 million ... "

– 13 –

Oscar got it wrong, Munch's figure not standing on a bridge but a path.
Bridge?
Path?
Both spaces of between with a difference between them.

A year after the massacre, Oscar is in London reading the *Evening Standard*:
"The gunman accused of killing 77 people in Norway's worst peacetime attack denounced the court today on the first day of his trial and gave a far-Right clenched fist salute in front of survivors and relatives of the dead."

Norway. 2012.
"As victims' families sobbed in the public gallery, Anders Breivik ... pleaded not guilty ... claiming he was acting in 'self-defense' against Islam and the country's ruling Labour Party."

Norway. Munch's poem. 1895.
"I was walking along a path with two friends — the sun was setting — suddenly the sky turned blood red — I paused, feeling exhausted and leaned on the fence —"

Norway. 2012.
" ... he placed a car bomb outside the government's main office building killing eight people ... at the Labour Party's summer youth camp on the nearby island Utoya, took 69 lives ... "

Norway. 1895.
"there was blood and tongues of fire above the blue-black fjord and the city."

Norway. 2012.
"Breivik broke into tears halfway through a viewing of his 12-minute movie ... an abridged version of his 1,500 page manifesto ... released shortly before ... his killing spree."

Norway. 1895.
"My friends walked on, and I stood there trembling with anxiety — and sensed an infinite scream passing through nature."

Part 19

Vancouver 2012

December and New Year holidays having just exhausted themselves. Oscar and her son are taking a stroll in their neighbourhood. It's a monochromatic afternoon — Commercial Drive oddly quiet — idling between holiday and back to work. A rash of handmade 8½ x 11-inch posters affixed on windows, walls, poles draws Oscar's attention.

gold hoodie
Friday,
November 18th, 2011

white and blue
checkered
dress shirt
December 16th, 2011

One after another, Oscar is unable to ignore each set of eyes looking at the intimate who took the photo before …

brown eyes (has been known
to wear coloured contacts)
May, 2011

For blocks and blocks they are everywhere. All are duplicates except one that only appears once. Her thirteen-year-old son remains thankfully oblivious.

black polo shoes
with white trim
Thursday,
August 18th, 2011

The angst of the intimates who made these posters, affixed
them everywhere deposits itself in Oscar.

                              navy T-shirt
                              Tuesday,
                              January 17th, 2011

Oscar's chest tightens with the jolt of how suddenly a life is
reduced to descriptions of personal effects, details of body,
location of last seen. The descriptive texts are so formulaic they
quickly become a litany.

The relief of closing a door.

Oscar makes her son's favourite lunch of butter pasta but feels
her shoulders cinch as another door opens — memories of
how he almost disappeared during the first month of his life in
intensive care. After dishes, Oscar makes up an excuse that she
forgot to buy rapini. Tells him she'll be back in twenty minutes.
Writes down her mobile number by the phone. Reminds him
not to answer the door.

Takes her smartphone. And notepad.

–2–

                    20-year-old African Canadian
                          gold hoodie
                        grey baseball cap
                with white & red "OBEY" logo

                                   25-year-old
                                   white and blue
                                         checkered
                                         dress shirt
                                   Athletic Build

28-year-old Quatsino First Nations
brown eyes (has been known
to wear coloured contacts)
        long brown hair
(has been known to dye hair)

                19-year-old Filipino
                black
                polo shoes with white trim
                Height: 5'10",
                Weight: 160–170 lbs

                                34-year-old Caucasian
                                navy T-shirt
                                no tattoos or
                                piercing

gold hoodie
known to take hikes or ...
long urban walks ... unusual
behaviour
not to return home

white and blue
checkered
dress shirt
disappearance is
entirely out of character
and a complete mystery

brown eyes (has been known
to wear coloured contacts)
tips regarding
if you wish to
remain anonymous ...

black polo shoes with
white trim
was not wearing his
eyeglasses

navy T-shirt
hasn't
been
seen
or heard of
since

MISSING
gold hoodie

FOUND
(May 2, 2012, in a small creek above Norvan Falls ... dental
records confirmed his identity ... ruled his death an
accident)

MISSING
white and blue checkered dress shirt

FOUND
(body was found December 31, 2013, submerged
beneath Quayside Marina dock, cause of death
"undetermined")

MISSING
brown eyes (has been known to wear coloured contacts)

FOUND
(May 29, 2014, family made another plea, "She was the life of
our family ... we're never going to give up.")
*May 1, 2014, the *Globe and Mail*,
"Police have compiled nearly 1,200 cases of murdered or missing
aboriginal women."

MISSING
black polo shoes with white trim

FOUND
(no further information)

MISSING
navy T-shirt

FOUND
(March 10, 2012, the human remains found in the woods near
Alpine Meadows ... foul play does not appear to be a
factor)

Part 20

Montreal, Vancouver, Iowa, Edmonton 2012

The head is found.

(his head)

Four days after finishing *Oscar of Between*, Part 18, Oscar is sketching out possible beginnings for Parts 19 and 20. To lessen the shrill of a table saw nearby, she has CBC's *Tempo* on and finds herself suddenly in the hourly news top story:

In Montreal, a police dog has located "what appear to be human remains that may be a head."

[shock]

Found on an anonymous tip: "tip, a piece or attachment to be fitted to the end of something."

In a park.

By a pond.

Before the news came on, Oscar had just written this: "Rahat's manuscript consult with Oscar. Rahat working on a memoir about being a Muslim in Canada pre-9/11 and post-9/11."

Then in *CBC News* real time:
" … police dog … may be a head."

[pause]

Recently back from Berlin, Oscar comments to Rahat that strategies of camouflage promote forgetting. And although she has no direct connection to the Second World War, it seems to be in Oscar's DNA, and she'd wanted to go to Berlin for years; needed to draw closer to its reality.

Rahat's eyes shift to Oscar's:

"We can never stop reading about World War II."

"Yes. Never."

– 3 –

A couple of weeks prior, Oscar in extended phone conversation with her dear friend Cheryl.

Oscar in Vancouver.

Cheryl in Toronto.

Among the array of topics, they always discuss their work. Oscar observes that her manuscript keeps returning to violence. Cheryl asks what her thinking is about this. Oscar grasps at a couple of reasons but says she is taking her time in articulating why.

Cheryl, who has been making numerous bodies of work over the past fourteen years comprised of frame grabs from surveillance Web cams and home cams remarks that all our systems rely on various forms of aggressive control, threat and underlying violence.

Oscar: "And none of this will change if women remain silent."

Summer, 2012. Oscar. In Edmonton. At the *Precarious Theorizing Symposium* at the University of Alberta: an idea/emotion-infused gathering to honour and continue the thinking of Dr. Sharon Rosenberg, who died two years prior. Sharon had sought out Oscar as an editorial consultant for her increasingly unconventional scholarly writing not long before she was diagnosed. Two of Sharon's central concerns were "traumatic ignorance" and "memorialization of violent deaths."

Oscar, preparing for the conference, fails (once again) to turn down the volume before the CBC's top news story begins: "Seventy-two people have been shot while attending the new Batman movie — twelve are already confirmed dead. The shooter is an unidentified young man who wore combat gear."

Oscar. Stopped. In. Her. Tracks.

A few days later, Oscar decides to conclude her keynote with a reading from *Oscar of Between*, Part 18.

No one stirs after she finishes.

It is utterly silent.

Oscar, still looking down, gathers herself. Sighs. Looks up at their faces.

"I feel an urge to apologize but I am not going to. I know that was hard to hear but we are living in troubling times. Very troubling times."

[pause]

A tender clapping falls on them all like much-needed rain.

– 6 –

The next day at the final presentations, two women scholars of German origin comment on their struggle to reconcile themselves to the Second World War.

One of the women reflects: "How could it be that amidst all of our theorizing what we weren't doing ... was ... talking about our own trans-generational hauntings?"

Sharon was Jewish.

The other woman says that the possibility, even assumption, of being implicated leaves her feeling frustrated and hopeless: "Where can you go with that?"

Oscar agrees that "implicated" and "complicit" are accurate, but that they also stall us in various forms of reactivity.

She searches for another word.

Then it surfaces:
"Disassociation.
This is what deeply concerns me — its deadly toll on us all."

Part 21

Vancouver 2012

For two weeks Oscar cannot bear to return to her manuscript. Cannot even look at it. Sadness overwhelms her. Yes, there are other factors (concerns about health, loneliness) but it still comes back to *Oscar of Between*.

It comforts her when she recalls how she could only write *Bloodroot* every other month. Had to alternate it with working on other writing. That was the only way Oscar could navigate the intensity of *Bloodroot*; stay faithful to what it required.

In Part 20, Oscar recalled the conversation with Rahat. By the end of writing that section — the Denver massacre. Since then, the Sikh Temple massacre. Milwaukee, Wisconsin. Six Sikhs killed. Others seriously wounded. The gunman a former army man.

When will the officials stop calling these "isolated incidents"?

When will people stop saying, "It's not my problem"?

"Theatre of war" normalized into "theatre of public" thinking.

Violence-based entertainment and narratives our bread and butter.

She did write a few pages. Trying to find a middle ground. But it seems to continue to shift away beneath her feet. On the phone with Myrna, Oscar describes her new workshop about writing into and out of the between and Myrna asks her who are her companions in that. Immediately, Jonina, Renee and Rahat come to mind. Jonina writing about growing up in the shadows of being Métis and Icelandic. Renee, writing about the Air India Flight 182 bombing in which her aunt and uncle died. And Rahat, writing about her experiences growing up as a South Asian Canadian Muslim pre- and post-9/11. Jonina, Renee, Rahat: writers knowing what's at stake and not backing away from it.

Part 22

Hornby Island, Vancouver 2012

Three years ago (November 2009) when Oscar wrote "*Oscar, Part 15*," she left something out.

· Something happened.

Happened after Arleen returned home. Oscar had planned to stay on to write for two more days. She'd stayed at Deb's cottage before: was at home there.

After Arleen left Oscar was oddly fidgety. Couldn't settle down to write. Became increasingly anxious.

By mid-afternoon, a sentence inserted itself into her mind:

" A woman on Hornby is going to be killed." .

It was imminent. How imminent Oscar couldn't tell. What to do? Drive around the island yelling out the window: "Watch out! A woman is going to be murdered"?

No one would take her seriously. Oscar could scarcely take herself seriously. It persisted: it was going to happen. There was nothing she could do to prevent it.

By late afternoon, she sensed it had some connection to Deb's cottage. That night she slept little. Left the island on the first morning ferry.

–2–

A couple of months later, Oscar runs into Deb at a Writer's Studio reading.

"Did you have a good time writing at the cottage?"

Deb seems fine so all must be well. "We had a great time! As you know, it's the perfect place for a writing retreat."

Hesitation hangs between them — Deb's face of anticipation waits for Oscar's next words.

Embarrassed but not wanting to appear ungrateful, Oscar admits she had been afraid that something bad was going to happen and left early.

Deb's face clenches into grief.

Something bad had. TemPeSt Gale, a friend of hers, had recently been murdered. Her distraught parents were staying in Deb's cottage.

– 3 –

The next day Oscar goes online, reads a *Digital Journal* account: "900 residents live a tranquil life on Hornby Island … it is the first time anyone has been killed on this island paradise."

"Police questioned a person of interest visiting Hornby who had stalked Gale's father and mother to the point where they had sought shelter at a friend's house overnight."

Docked at the same marina, "he stalked her parents because he thought someone had spilled Coca-Cola on his boat."

– 4 –

TemPeSt — a vibrant twenty-five-year-old "beloved musician and entertainer" — had declined to join her parents that night. This was Hornby, after all.

Next morning she's not in her boat. She's in twenty feet water.
Face down.

— life less —

– 5 –

A year later, Oscar sees Deb and asks what has happened: has a
murderer been convicted?

"No, but … " [Oscar deletes something here for others' safety].

"I knew it was going to happen when I was at your cottage but
had absolutely no idea who was going to be killed."

Deb's taken aback.

"You *knew* when you were at the cottage?"

"Yeah. Didn't I tell you that?"

"No. You just told me about being uneasy and leaving because
you thought it had something to do with our place."

— the body as evidence —

(is not enough)

Part 23

Vancouver 2012

– 1 –

Oscar and Nancy are driving out to Pitt Meadows to check on Nancy's property there. As they drive Highway 1 Nancy comments in the midst of their drifting conversation that Oscar is "quite hidden" as a person.

"That surprises me. I'd like to ask you more about that later when we're not driving."

When walking on Nancy's land by the Pitt River, Oscar asks Nancy to elaborate. She replies that although Oscar is a warm and present person, it takes time for Oscar to reveal more about herself. "Unlike me," Nancy laughs, "who blurts everything out!"

– 2 –

Later, Oscar reflects on her tendency to not assume others' interest, that her deepest wound is that of not being heard. This, in turn, fuels her desire to inquire and listen deeply to others — as much as she's able — as it's often enlightening. It does strike her that it is rare for the other person to ask her deeper questions in return. *That* is a precious encounter.

– 3 –

It's a mid-morning November chill-grey day accented with still some splashes of orange and yellow when the phone rings. Oscar, immersed in revising a section of this manuscript, pauses; considers whether to check call display. Oscar isn't one to routinely answer the phone but something makes her jump up and catch the call on the last ring. The call is from Ottawa but the display doesn't illuminate who the caller is.

"Hello, Betsy?"

"Yes."

"It's Marion calling. I am about to send out the applications to the juries and I want to ask you about your application — I don't think you have applied to the right jury."

"I don't understand."

"I am thinking your application belongs in another jury and I want to discuss it with you."

"Are you the literary officer?"

"Yes, I am sorry, I didn't clarify that."

"Okay. Marion, I've spent twenty years applying to either the poetry jury or the nonfiction jury and both have repeatedly doubted that my writing fits their genre. It has been utterly demoralizing. In fact, as I understood it from the previous literary officer, this problem with those juries' expectations is partly what prompted this new Exploratory Writing Jury. Please don't move my application to another jury!"

[What if Oscar hadn't picked up the phone?]

They talk more candidly, with a careful listening on both of their parts, despite the fact that they are complete strangers.

"Yes, in looking at the writing sample you submitted I can now see it would not suit either of the other juries."

[They say goodbye.]

Oscar hangs up, her whole being vibrating with alertness at how close she came to going down that dead-end path again.

Part *24*

Toronto, Newtown 2012

Oscar meets Mark at the Utopia in Little Italy. It's been
a couple of years since they've seen each other yet their
conversation as usual ranges over a number of topics with
ease. As they talk, Oscar notices a blue neon sign across the
street that spells in perpendicular block letters **PSYCHIC** over
Mark's right shoulder and over his left, the end of a sign that
says **OCCASION**. Oscar mentions that the ancient Greeks
had rejected reading text when it was first introduced to the
populous. They found it a limiting experience compared to
reading the world — from moment to moment — around
them. Consequently, penalties were introduced that forced
them to adapt. Oscar and Mark shift to talking about how the
experience of deep reading seems to be rapidly decreasing as
digital reading is increasing.

Later, in Sellers & Newel Second-Hand Books, they fan out
to scan the shelves and Oscar finds and purchases *Inside Hitler's
Bunker: The Last Days of the Third Reich*. They meet at the front
of the store and Oscar mentions *A Woman in Berlin*. Mark
recalls a rivetting three-hour film he saw about Hitler's last
days in the Führerbunker. She shows Mark the book she just
bought and they simultaneously notice the small print at the
bottom of the cover: "Inspiration for the Oscar-nominated film,
Downfall" and Mark reels slightly: "That's the movie I was just
describing!"

Oscar picks up her son's one-word text message to her:

"Why?"

She's just boarded the train for Montreal after teaching a
writing workshop in Toronto. Had only heard about the Sandy
Hook Elementary School massacre in Newtown late last night.

Had difficulty sleeping. Just wanted to jump on the next plane to wrap her arms around him. In the workshop yesterday, she had referred to the section of *Oscar* about the Norwegian massacre in 2011 and the recent Denver massacre. Here it was again: this time grade one children and their teachers.

Last night, Andrea and Oscar talked before they tried to turn in for the night. Oscar feeling urgency: "There's something terribly wrong in our culture but we refuse to seriously address it because it's too profitable." Andrea (a high school teacher) concurring that kids are suffering but nothing of any consequence is being done. Just last week Oscar had had a long conversation with her son about FB bullying among some of his classmates.

– 3 –

The twenty-year-old, "bright but remote," dressed in camouflage, shot his mother — who was a "gun enthusiast" — in the face several times. Then, he took "the guns belonging to her," drove to the school to repeatedly shoot and kill twenty first-graders, six women on staff and, as the police arrived, himself.

– 4 –

The bravery of these women. Two attempted to tackle him "in order to protect their students" and were killed. Another hid her students in her classroom's closets and cabinets then met him at the door; told him they were in the gym.

He killed her. Continued on down the hall.

Part 25

Vancouver 2013

Oscar began referring to herself as a "recovering romantic" sometime after her second big break-up — break-a-way, break-into, breakneck, break-through, breakdown, break-apart — it was some of all of these. Two twelve-year, back-to-back lesbian relationships, both fuelled by a potent mix of sense of family and artistic interface. Both aberrant relationships within the literary community complicated by silent judgement and loyalties.

Now in her ninth year on her own, seeking another way, Oscar wonders: Have I recovered from romance's illusions, its spectacular wounds?

– 2 –

Vancouver's Dead Poets' Reading Series. Oscar a featured poet invited to read from a deceased poet's work held in esteem. Oscar chooses Adrienne Rich's collections.

Collision/emotions.

Rich's 1976 *Twenty-One Love Poems* flung open the door of lesbian desire in the public world:

> "No one has imagined us. We want to live like trees,
> Sycamores blazing through the sulphuric air,
> dappled with scars, still exuberantly budding,
> our animal passion rooted in the city."

Oscar and Daphne ablaze on a cross-country book tour reading from their erotically charged books.

The 1980s and '90s: these were exhilarating, anything-is-possible in feminist literary production and publishing years. Then racism, classism and homophobia, augmented by withdrawal of funding grants, put us into a tailspin.

Then, with the advent of Canadian big-box bookstores in 1997, small feminist and literary bookstores began closing.

2003. Shock. Press Gang (a major feminist publisher) bankrupt. Rita and Oscar organize the Press Gang Authors Benefit Reading.

The Western Front is packed.

Below, the sidewalk is filled with those who couldn't get in but refuse to leave. After each set, the authors go down and give their reading again.

During the intermission, several younger feminist writers seek Oscar out, saying: "This is amazing! Why doesn't this happen more often?"

Oscar replies: "We used to have big readings like this all the time."

Puzzlement passes over their faces
                           — Oscar taken aback —

so few years have passed and it's as if
it never happened.

Adrienne's earlier collections reignite that intoxicating time when poetry was as elemental as air.

As Oscar reads through all of Rich's collections, in *The Dream of a Common Language* she feels she's stumbled upon a letter written by a beloved and realizes how much she's missed Adrienne.

Palpable. Rich's fierce engagement with the reader. As she voices Rich's poems there is an intense sensation of I–need–to–hear–this in the room and Oscar tremors.

> "Silence can be a plan
> Rigorously executed
>
> the blueprint for a life
>
> It is a presence
> It has a history   a form
>
> Do not confuse it
> With any kind of absence"

Part 26

Montreal 2013

The room, once white, is still white enough to converse with daylight. The room's shape suits Oscar: two walls traditional right-angled walls; one wall starts off conventionally but after the doorway veers left, then straightens into a short wall just big enough to accommodate a pair of rectangular windows. The view is of a terracotta brick wall veined with dormant ivy and a V of clothesline strung from the backyard pole to Denis' and his neighbour's facing porches. When Oscar props herself up, she gazes across the back laneway to the brick three-storey walk-ups with spiral staircases topped with the unambiguous blue Montreal sky. Oscar relishes the luxury of lying in bed, observing all the petite narratives that transpire heedlessly there.

The room's familiars are simple:

a small white set of drawers; a white and black director's chair; a small closet on the left wall. The floor is original, varnished pine.

After her initial elation at being back in Montreal, sleep eludes Oscar. At 2 a.m. she turns on the light; opens *Orlando: A Biography*. It's been decades since she read it. Only recently did it strike her that Oscar and Orlando may be literary companions. It's a pocketbook. 1977 Panther Granada edition. The paper is coarse and browned with time. She reads the first page, a short biography. The sentence, "Recurring bouts of madness plagued both her childhood and married life and in April 1941 Virginia Woolf took her life," startles Oscar with its confident use of the term "madness." Then she thinks of her visit to Monk's House last spring — how peaceful it was, how at home she felt.

On the preface page, Oscar puzzled that Woolf's extensive acknowledgements don't mention Vita. She flips to the next page:

To V. Sackville-West.

Immediately below is an inscription in blue ink. Oscar begins to turn the page. Assumes it's a secondhand book that's inscribed to a stranger but the handwriting's jaunty slant upward catches her eye. She looks closer. Reads. Is taken aback. It's inscribed to her.

> Betsy,
> To my well-loved friend in celebration
> of a new joy!
>   Sally

Oscar rereads the inscription. Sally? Then it sinks in. Toronto. The '70s. Sally was Oscar's dear friend who believed in Oscar as a writer; edited some of her early poems. Three decades older than Oscar, Sally lamented the sheer proliferation of books since the turn of the century that made it no longer possible to read all the classics in one's lifetime. Oscar's first book dedicated to Sally. Included a suite of poems about Sally's death.

Now. In the middle of this sleepless night, Oscar holds this trace of Sally in her hands. A sob gathers inside but cannot find its way out.

Oscar. Too stunned to cry. Stunned by how written words have a life a logic a will of their own, an eerie sense of their own timing.

What did Sally's reference to "new joy!" mean? Think context. Then Oscar gets it. It's a reference to Oscar falling in love with J, her first soft-lipped lover.

Earlier that evening, when reading *Camouflage* (the book accompanying the Imperial War Museum's exhibit), Oscar notices a connection she hasn't before:

" … the range of these early guns was not long enough to enable soldiers to hide and fire at the same time. This changed with the invention of the rifle."

Facing off in close range, side by side in opposing lines of bright-coloured uniforms, firing volley after volley until "one side decided it had had enough and ran" morphed into unpredictable proximities, stealth, stalking, surprise attacks.

The rifle = distance = camouflage = disassociation.
Drones.

– 4 –

Oscar's favourite reverie time
: after-breakfast tea.

[pause]

Oscar wonders why we writers so seldom evoke the interior spaces we live and write in when they shape and influence our daily lives so thoroughly.

[pause]

The grey cat is back! Oscar's been looking for it since arriving two days ago — it, of course, not being back but Oscar herself is back. The grey cat, like Montaigne, daily observes the neighbourhood's quotidian and archives it all in its brain.

It never seems to lessen: how precious these writing times in Denis' flat are. And in Maxine's flat in London. A number of years ago, Oscar contacted each of them about doing a flat exchange. Over the years, she has grown to tenderly know them via occupying their appartments: their preferences and comforts; their private logic and habits. Only secondarily has Oscar learned of them in person, during brief overlaps.

Although Oscar cherishes her den, it is where she spends most of her time working on other writers' manuscripts. This is the site of only her writing. Too, it reminds her of one of her girlhood strategies: building secret "forts" in the barnyard and surrounding woods and fields where she could do more than maintain and endure; where she could reside.

– 5 –

"The interior of the rifle barrel was created with spiral grooves so the bullet revolved in the air as it left the gun. Because of this it offered great improvements in accuracy and range compared with the smoothbore musket ... A revolution in tactics followed."

" ... the bullet revolved in the air ... "

"A revolution in tactics followed."

Then, in 1942, the Nazis invented the MG42 machine gun that fired 1,200 to 1,500 rounds per minute.

– 6 –

Librairie Le Port de tête on Mont-Royal: Carla Harryman reading from her new book *Adorno's Noise*, Gail Scott presiding. Carla reads from "Headless Heads." Oscar reverberates. Shifts, spreads her knees apart to rest forearms on thighs. Looks down at the old pine floor.

Carla's riffing off everything from Max Ernst's *La femme 100 têtes!* to Blake's. *The Ghost of a Flea* to Richter's painting *Betty* (model for head on butcher's paper his daughter). Oscar punctuated by the Luka Magnotta inquiry into the dismemberment of Concordia student Lin Jin that began this week.

Magnotta charged with "mailing the body parts across the country."

The depravity of this act.

On the second day of the inquiry, Lin Jin's father was escorted from the courtroom due to an emission from his mouth: sobbing.

– 7 –

"The birth of modern camouflage was a direct consequence of the invention of the aeroplane."

— aerial reconnaissance —

It was now possible to make an inventory of the enemy's position, vehicles, artillery, number of soldiers.

— deception became the most lethal of weapons —

"This process led to a deadly game of hide-and-seek … each side disguise[d] any build-up … [to] retain the advantage of surprise before any major offensive."

Summer of 1918, Parisian portraitist and white kid-gloved dandy Lucien-Victor Guirand de Scévola became the first camoufleur.

He was put in charge of camouflage workshops along the Western Front "employing 1,200 men and 8,000 women."

– 8 –

She's been hit — engine cuts out/propeller clock hands stop — skirmish recedes as Oscar spirals out of control (wings cutting through air the only sound).

The Spitfire's litheness mesmerizes Oscar as it gyres to the sea.

Together. They go down. Together.

This memory came out of the blue some twenty years ago.

– 9 –

Once, when she was hesitant to enter some teenage activity her father was driving her to, he gave her a tip:

"Just walk in like you belong there."

Tactics. Her father knew. Gave this rare camo cue to Oscar.

Part 27

Montreal 2013

– 1 –

It happens.

Happens after twenty years of writing; twenty years of applying; twenty years of "Unfortunately(s) … "

It happens on a sunny Montreal day as the magic realism of the storm's creations begin to melt. On this twentieth day of March 2013 day: the spring equinox. This day when the length between sunrise and sunset/sunset and sunrise is exactly the same. It happens on this one day of perfect betweenness. Oscar receives the call.

She got the writing grant.

– 2 –

A few nights ago when Oscar began reading *Orlando*, Woolf had her laughing out loud by the third page:

"He was describing, as all poets are for ever describing, nature, and in order to match the shade of green precisely he looked (and here he showed more audacity than most) at the thing itself, which happened to be a laurel bush growing beneath the window. After that, of course, he could write no more. Green in nature was one thing, green in literature another. Nature and letters seem to have a natural antipathy: bring them together and they tear each other to pieces."

When Oscar was more than twice Orlando's years, she too was seized by green. Wrote the suite of green ("the greed, the gulp of green" and "who could ever speak green?") in her book *only this blue*.

Two nights ago Lise and Oscar saw the FIFA documentary on American composer John Cage, a pioneer of indeterminacy in music. Indeterminacy hand-in-hand with First World War.

Oscar was intrigued to find that Cage thought of himself more as a listener than a composer (Oscar thinks of herself in this way too). In *4'33"*, Cage's most ground-breaking composition, musicians and audience sit "silently" at the ready for the concert, only to gradually discover that the music is the soundscape they are in.

Cage a practitioner of Zen.

As she writes, Oscar waits. A lot. And listens. Often listens far more of the time than inscribing. She never knows where the sounds, rhythms, language, movement of the line, image, thought or narrative will take her just as she never really knows from moment to moment where life will take her. Surrenders again. And, again.

Although Oscar listens and tunes each line as she writes, she seldom looks back and rereads until she's completed the first draft. Then she's curious to engage with it anew. She does revise a piece intensively when asked by a publication for some work. This, however, is the exception.

Unlike her inscribing method, not looking back is not true to life.

Or, is it? Bits of previous experience unpredictably surface in our memory mostly of their own will, not ours.

Last summer, while house-sitting at Clarissa's and preparing her grant application, Oscar did sit down and read what she had written thus far: Parts 1–20. She was relieved to find how much it engaged her, held together narratively. Then she promptly forgot most of it.

– 5 –

It's difficult to follow when you think that you already know the way.

– 6 –

Cage was devoted to listening to chance and ambient sounds infusing our daily life. Compositional form was given by the circumstance and specific spatiality these sounds took place in, or by random patterns based on the solid and broken lines determined by throwing the coins of the *I Ching*. His atypical compositions necessitated that he invent new ways of creating musical score notation.

For Cage, improvisational music was an illusion, simply a reconfiguration of what the musician had already played, heard, knew.

Part 28

Montreal 2013

– 1 –

The Plateau. Instantaneous positioning. French-speaking (or not).

Although it must also be said that prowess of gender marking and signalling remains skilfully refined in Montreal.

And, although Oscar is not routinely taken for a man here, she frequently is.

Camouflage enables efficiency. Assumptions get things done.

Unthinkingly.

– 2 –

If you suppose that gender protocol and positioning in daily encounters between strangers is nearly obsolete, you are mistaken.

When: a stranger sincerely apologizes for bumping into Oscar;

a bank teller is unusually attentive and solicitous;

a woman next to Oscar on a plane asks a series of genuine questions about Oscar's professional life;

a clutch of girls on the sidewalk moves aside when Oscar is approaching, or the bus driver has no qualms about letting her off at an undesignated stop;

a woman is considering what to buy in a produce section suddenly moves aside with apology;

a boy's arm mid-air with snowball halts to check Oscar's eyes for possible threat as she walks by;

the extent of deferential treatment never ceases to astonish her.

– 3 –

The Internet is rampant with all sorts of camouflage and anonymous shaming, vicious GTFO and sexual and violent messages sent to female gamers.

Big Data collection corporations on average have 18,000 pieces of information culled from every aspect of our online activities to sell to other corporation marketing departments. Big Data's cannibalizing of our habits and preferences is becoming the world's most valuable and profitable resource.

Big Data refuses to disclose its information on us, to us. Harmful misinformation is almost impossible to correct.

For Big Data (echo of Big Daddy), anonymity on our computers, our handheld devices is a ruse.

– 4 –

A Woman in Berlin: Eight Weeks in the Conquered City by Anonymous, published in 1959, when anonymity was still an option.

– 5 –

The gender-specific necessity of camouflage.

In the book's foreword, written by the publisher who eventually reprinted it in 2001, he writes:

"By the seventies ... photocopies of the text ... began to circulate in Berlin among the radical students of 1968 and the burgeoning women's movement."

When he searched for the author during the mid-1980s, he discovered that the "author could not be traced, the original publisher had disappeared, and it was not clear who held the copyright ... "

Eventually he tracked down the original publisher's widow who knew the diarist. She interceded and spoke with the author who still did not want her identity to ever be revealed, nor did she want the book to be reprinted while she was still alive.

After her death in 2001, he reprinted the book.

– 6 –

Oscar eats her favourite meal of the day (breakfast) as she reads the *New York Times*. March 16, 2013:

A former executive vice-president of global corporate affairs for Kraft Food writes:

" ... the food industry knows it has a problem, potentially a very big one if the forces against it ever do coalesce effectively. So, in maneuvering for protection by managing public opinion and policy formation, the industry will always try to camouflage itself as just another one of the many causes for the growth of obesity. Just as the National Rifle Association points to mental illness and violent video games as a way to deflect attention from the inherent dangers of guns ... We shouldn't fall for it."

Part 29

Vancouver, Berlin 2013

– 1 –

A year ago: Oscar and Ingrid in Berlin. Upon arriving, Oscar struck by there being only red and green traffic lights — yellow (the between) non-existent — Oscar speculating this signalled an underlying black or white mentality.

Just now, Oscar recalls an anecdote Shaena told her after Oscar returned from her trip. Shaena's friend, a resident of Berlin for many years, had been playing Frisbee with his German girlfriend in one of the parks. After they had finished and had settled on a blanket to picnic, a few young immigrant men began playing Frisbee close by. To his surprise, his girlfriend told them: "Go away ... you can't play here. This is *our park.*"

– 2 –

Mid-afternoon, downtown Vancouver congestion.

Oscar, wearing her burnished gold-chartreuse biking shell, is trying to find the bike path to the West End. Unnerved. The supposed bike lane is nowhere in sight.

Just as the yellow switches to red, Oscar cuts in front of an idling car that simultaneously begins to accelerate; then halts. She waves thanks and mouths "sorry." As she retreats to the sidewalk, a male driver on the intersecting street yells:

"You stupid idiot!"

His reaction surprises Oscar. She nods a yes-you-are-right but then retorts, "It's fine!" for it was now. Peddling on, her next reaction was the most unexpected one:

surge of exhilaration!

Over the course of her life, all the unacknowledged, unsaid undercurrents about her betweenness denied outright but mostly camouflaged. To have it spontaneously shouted at her and to shout back was refreshing. Yet, she also realizes she is safe, she is not a young Black man who could have been as easily shot.

– 3 –

A few minutes later, peddling through the traffic-calmed streets of the West End, Oscar realizes: "He thought I was a guy. That's why he was so direct."

Part 30

Vancouver, Berlin, Victoria 2013

Orlando. Returns to England from Constantinople
Ambassadorship and her subsequent time with the Thessalian
hills gypsies. Upon arriving at her country estate a "whole
retinue of servants" welcomes her home.

Orlando. Indisputably Orlando yet not ... Mrs. Grimsditch
curtseys, gasps:

"Milord! Milady! Milady! Milord!"

Then, "no one showed an instant's suspicion" (they being
British and being servants). Even Orlando's dogs suffered not
a hair's width of confusion, "for the dumb creatures ... are far
better judges of identity and character than we are."

– 2 –

A year ago in Berlin, Oscar and Ingrid looked for some
trousers for Oscar: Oscar's an ambivalent shopper in the
extreme.

Soon, Oscar was enervated. "That's it — no more shopping."

A block or two later Oscar's eyes caught sight of a pair in a
small shop window. They headed in. Few minutes later, chuffed
that she's succeeded, Oscar asked Ingrid to take her picture. As
Oscar moved toward the store window she noticed its name

:Oskar's.

Mid-morning East Van sidewalk, men sit at small tables in front of Abruzzo's old-style Italian cappuccino bar. At the far end, an older man by himself is sizing up Oscar as she strides comfortably along. She does not avert her eyes from his stare and he knows she's watching his eyes move slowly down her body

— decision —

                        still look back at him, look down,

or, say something to pivot it?

She remembers she is wearing her new men's Italian sandals and says to him:

             "Like my shoes?"

His eyes flash up to her face.

                [pause]

Then he gives her the thumbs up.

Joanne is asking what *Oscar of Between* is about. Oscar sketches the invention of camouflage in the First World War through to absorption of it in "civilian" lives and increasing violence. Mentions an interview with the wrestling teammate of Boston Bomber Dzhokhar Tsarnaev. His shock. Now feared any friend might be a terrorist; that he wouldn't have a clue until something terrible happened.

Oscar tells Joanne of a recent US study that reveals Americans recognize physical acts of bravery as courageous but are unable to recognize, or are indifferent to or suspicious of, moral acts of courage.

Joanne nods.

Oscar's been house-sitting for her friend Clarissa. After waiting nine months for access to a clothesline and a sunny day, she's just hung out the handmade quilt her grandmother sewed for Oscar's future wedding present when she was still young. Clarissa's house is densely populated with mementoes, paintings and photos that span five generations of her family. Oscar has a handful that span three generations. Oscar's lineage is mostly stored in gestures like hanging the laundry outdoors. Until now, this has only been an option when she's at Denis' in Montreal. This morning, she inhales the ozone timelessness of it, quietly delights in her understanding of how to judge the weather, right time of day, which direction to face certain items, how to consider distribution of weight (know where to pin the heavier and lighter ones), how to maximize use of limited space (socks between legs of pants), while she savours the sparkling allegro of the house sparrow; anticipates the heady mix of sun and garden fragrance-infused dried clothes when she will slip into bed that night.

Oscar leaning into writing about Newtown first grader Ben Wheeler's grieving parents who spoke with such gentle intelligence about the urgent need for Americans to stop stockpiling weapons, or, leaning into her agitation about the twenty-something-year-old Germans (cans of beer in hand) giggling as they played hide-and-seek in the Holocaust Memorial, or, leaning into Orlando's belief "No passion is stronger in the breast of man than the desire to make others believe as he believes." But, no. This morning Oscar writes about the art of drying clothes outdoors, passed down to her from the long line of women.

Part 31

Vancouver, Toronto, Mexico 2013

June 8, 2013. Vancouver. Oscar invited to read at the 23rd
Annual Virginia Woolf Conference banquet — between the
entree and dessert.

Of all her betweennesses, this is a new challenge for Oscar.

She considers. A palate cleanser? Something refreshing,
humorous (the typical fare) but this is not Oscar's forte.

Oscar flummoxed. Every idea of what to read nosedives like an
inadequately made paper airplane.

Then Orlando taps her on the shoulder.

There's the fit: Orlando and Oscar — food, drink, lively
exchange of ideas.

Oscar picks up the book, begins to flip through it when this
passage catches her eye:

"Orlando? still the Orlando she needs may not come; these
selves of which we are built up, one on top of another, as
plates are piled on a waiter's hand, have attachments elsewhere,
sympathies, little constitutions and rights of their own."

The romp and range of Virginia's intoxicating mind.

Yes. That's it! Orlando and Oscar.

Between! Between! Between!

Preparing for her reading, Oscar carefully turns the pages as she
searches for tasty bits. The book's spine has deteriorated — its
pages about to come loose. *Orlando* quotes here and there jump
off the page into conversation with Oscar.

Exhilarating. Done!

Oscar closes the book. Clears the table for dinner. Notices a strange sprinkle of yellow-gold particles where she had been working. On closer inspection, she realizes they're dried glue particles from the book's spine.

They look exactly like pollen.

– 2 –

Oscar. That first kiss. 1978. Toronto. Array of hardwood trees in their October colours vibrating in the clear-crisp night. J and Oscar. Strolling and talking; talking and strolling downtown. Drawn to each other in a way neither had known before. Pause in the middle of the green oval in front of Hart House as U of T students move through the night as the crow flies. Oscar and J. Pause. In the middle of the green. Grow quiet. Turn. Face each other. Lips close. That first kiss. Unlike any other. Soft spiralling of mutual surrender; defenceless desire.

– 3 –

Twenty-five years spooling forward from this kiss. Three major relationships and then, Oscar retreats. Has been a recovering romantic for the past nine years. Been. On her own. Solitary. As she was in her growing-up years. Oscar. Needing to find another way. Needing to unlearn the romantic script stock lines, idealizations and expectations that obscure the vulnerabilities we end up being at the mercy of.

October 2013. Oscar in Vancouver at the reception before the
Virginia Woolf Conference banquet. Oscar nervous "in the
extreme" (*Orlando*). As Oscar walks into the hotel convention
lobby, she spots Miranda and Sharon (who's also reading)
huddled together by Helen, the conference chair. Helen offers
to buy them a drink. Oscar confesses she's socially inept in these
situations, to which Miranda and Sharon confess similar feelings.

Oscar, who never socializes, eats nor drinks before a reading is
doing all three. Hopes for the best for her reading is at least an
hour and a half away.

Prior to the first course, Sharon reads from her book *Pair
of Scissors*. The audience is astute and responsive to Sharon's
elegant, witty riff on *Mrs. Dalloway*. Oscar relaxes. Some.

Salad, animated conversation with Miranda and Sharon, then
entree. Finally, plates are cleared. Liquids topped up. It's time.
Helen's intro. Miranda's intro: Oscar now at the mic. Begins
reading her *Orlando* and *Oscar* alternating excerpts. Feels
the room cohere, being in it together. Deep concentration
punctuated by laughter at the humorous bits. When the
banquet is over, Helen says to Oscar: "You could have heard a
pin drop, even on this carpet!"

With the academy, and in her schooling prior, Oscar kept
herself at arm's length. Found the pursuit of knowledge
in those halls was predictably routinized, defensively
territorial, sorely lacking in authentic inquiry. In recent
years, corporatization intensifying the academy's commodity
approach. Oscar relishing the freedom of inquiry, surprising
confluences between her excerpts, her guests' posted work and
readers' comments in her online salon.

In this month's salon, Oscar posted an excerpt that included her reunion with her high school friends Margaret and Penny in Mexico two years ago. The similarities between their lives are few, yet something connects them beyond high school memories. On their second day Oscar realizes what it is. Directness. A characteristic in Midwest women that was non-existent then, and likely still is now.

–6–

Although Penny's and Margaret's lives are more conventional than Oscar's, neither is traditional. On the third morning, as Oscar came down the stairs for breakfast, Margaret determinedly stepped out from the study and stood at the landing: "What happened? I've just finished reading *Bloodroot* and you didn't say what happened after you went back for more tests about your breast."

[halt]

Time stalls above them with no place to light.

Oscar's been debating how to tell them but suddenly there's no more debating. It's now.

Instinctively, she takes Margaret's hands in hers and places them firmly where her breasts used to be.

Margaret startles. "Ahh!" Removes her hands.

Then replies with conviction. "I've already thought about it. If I ever have breast cancer, I'm going to do the same thing."

[pause]

Then. They erupt. Into laughter about the bizarre exchange they've just had.

Part 32

Victoria, Iowa 2013

– 1 –

Victoria, mid-July, 2013. Oscar familiar with Victoria; has numerous friends here but this a new here she's been plunged into: a house-sit with a massive garden to tend and bee hives to navigate. On Acton Street in an enclave of houses shored up by large Garry oaks on all sides. Their prehistoric reptilian bark and dense, leafy clusters at the ends of their branches comfort Oscar. Garry oak grow only on the West Coast and its companion islands.

– 2 –

Two large hives. Oscar and bees gingerly becoming acquainted. When they buzz around her (don't bat them away!) she hums the note they make and this seems to ease their uncertainty. She watches their typical fourteen-hour workday: constant stream of ninety-degree angle ascent and descent to and from control tower hives. Two days ago, after house and garden orientation tour, Merrie-Ellen, Christopher and Oscar chatted. Christopher, a composer, has a garden studio adjacent to the beehives. Oscar delights in the bees' music and tells them of an Oregon seaside indigenous plant that opens its flowers to only one kind of bee to pollinate; a bee that changes its note to a frequency the flower prefers: middle C.

To note each other accurately; be noted accurately: what we all long for.

– 3 –

Half an hour of hand watering done on the front garden and timer-set sprinkler set on the side garden, Oscar now having breakfast on the narrow back porch. Morning sun is angling in wherever it can find openings through the Garry oaks and house next door. The continuous ascents and descents of the bees catch morning light on their backs and look like shooting stars.

Thousands and thousands of leaves and petals a-flutter. Oscar is listening to Ann Southam's "Webster's Spin." It sounds remarkably like bee music.

– 4 –

The complexity of watering schedules and methodologies that initially overwhelmed Oscar now familiar in this here of here. Oscar doesn't begrudge the hour plus of watering required morn and eve. It instructs her in the garden's language.

– 5 –

For such large trees, these Garry oaks are considerate trees.

If you were to think of leaves as hair, the Garry oak is not a big hair tree but more a clustered-at-the-ends-of-its-branches pubic hair tree sharing sunlight with all in its surround.

– 6 –

Sitting at the round wood kitchen table with the top of the Dutch door open, Oscar gazes over the layers and layers of garden foliage, past the tall, greying wood fences to the largest Garry oak on the other side. It harbours moss in its lower bifurcating limbs' crotch and has arranged all its graceful limbs in an easterly orientation so its secondary limb can drink in the western light.

Oscar thinks of Orlando writing her poem "The Oak Tree" for 300 years, keeping the rolled-up manuscript on his chest, then later, between her breasts. Sometimes forgotten, sometimes delighted in, sometimes reviled, "The Oak Tree" Orlando's only companion to weather all the changes in life over 300 years.

When "The Oak Tree" was in its seventh edition and had become the source of much acclaim and controversy, Orlando vows that all this "was ill suited as could be to the thing itself — a voice answering a voice."

– 7 –

Orlando's vow. Oscar will hold to her chest for the rest of her life.

– 8 –

The Greater Victoria Highlands forest. Beth and Oscar have just had a silky swim in the intimate cupped hand of Eagle Lake. Beth's telling Oscar about her new writing project, "invented histories." She's questing for the way obfuscated memories are housed in bone marrow and cells from the beginning of her life, for this is her only option. She hasn't even a birth certificate. Beth's brought a copy of one of the poems for Oscar to read. It has a quiet, oracular feel that magnetizes Oscar. Beth comments on how these poems seem to bewilder other poet friends.

"I can relate to that!" Oscar replies.

"Oh, *yes!*" Beth responds.

"You mean to your new work?"

"No: *your* work."

This is so rarely acknowledged, Oscar checks.

"You've noticed that?"

"Totally."

"I'm most aware of it in a group reading. It feels like I am coming from such a different place than other writers."

"You are."

– 9 –

He was born December 23, 1918, in Ft. Dodge, Iowa.

Oscar was born December 27, 1946, in Ft. Dodge, Iowa.

After the attack on Pearl Harbor, he enlisted and was stationed on a Navy supply ship for fourteen months. Utterly bored, he repeatedly requested a transfer to a destroyer but his commander repeatedly denied his request. To counter numbing monotony, he began writing vignettes about the small dramas being played out on ship.

Discharged in December 1945, he returned to New York where he'd worked as an editor at *Reader's Digest*. Began writing *Mr. Roberts*. It sold over a million copies: he became "the toast of the New York literary scene." The 1948 stage version, starring Henry Fonda, "was a smash" success.

[WRITER'S BLOCK]

He died in his bathtub a year later.

[the family's shame]

His name was Thomas Heggen. He was an excised relative. Here, Oscar thinks of her mother's plan to take a razor blade and cut out twenty pages of Oscar's first book.

How, subsequently she never mentioned the existence of her other books to her parents.

Oscar knew nothing of Thomas Heggen.

Then, her brother Steven discovered a new book, *Ross and Tom: Two American Tragedies*. It was an account of two first-book-hit authors living in New York who soared. Stalled. Committed. Suicide.

Oscar gets the book. Inhales it.

Her facial resemblance with Thomas is startling.

Comprehends her parents' distrust of books.

Books can kill.

– 10 –

Ross and Tom was published in 1974.

Oscar was married in 1969.

Her husband of eight years' name?

Thomas.

– 11 –

Czeslaw Milosz said a writer in the family is the end of family.

Jamaica Kincaid said she writes about her family as if they were dead.

What do author and family have in common?

A book can bring us to our knees.

– 12 –

It has taken Oscar almost forty years to acknowledge in writing the other author in the family.

Thomas Heggen.

After writing this, Oscar prepares lunch. Feels a vast shadow of sadness fall over her.

Pauses.

She accepts the power of the book. This is not what sorrows her.

No. It's Thomas's aloneness.

And hers.

Part 33

Toronto 2013

Toronto. Rush hour beginning. Oscar on Bloor Street — steely cumulus clouds compacting air — rain soon to pelt down. Oscar walking for past couple of hours searching for postal outlet and looking for a weekly gift she sends in EXPRESS ENVELOPE to her son. Oscar. Aching to find her way into *Oscar of Between*: images, phrases, ideas, pulsating words have been circling in her head for past few days. Oscar. Eager to cross the threshold but there's always the question of how to? Must be discovered each time. Impatient with herself for taking so long yet reminding herself that she just finished the *Margento* essay and that, unlike being in Denis' flat near Plateau Mont-Royal, in Toronto she's having to learn a new neighbourhood. Then. It happens!

Having found the postal outlet, purchased EXPRESS ENVELOPE, she's walking back to the apartment amidst rush-hour-pedestrians push while trying to insert a five-dollar bill into her change purse when coins and TTC tokens spray out across sidewalk. An approaching young man with baseball cap askew shouts to girlfriend at his side:

"Hey. Watch out! This is the *latest scam*! Don't help him! It was on the news last night!"

Oscar. Squats to pick up coins and tokens, glances up at him as he stops to watch. Quick assessment. He decides. Crouches down and helps as people stream by on either side but continues on to his girlfriend:

"If you put your bag down to help them, they grab it *and take off*!"

Toronto. Bloor at Ossington. 5:13 p.m. It happens! Torturing array of images, words, ideas begin to connect.

Oscar crosses the threshold.

Next morn. Oscar having encountered Oscar now shy around
Oscar, so tempted by distractions. To focus herself, Oscar gives
her self the advice she gave to her students in the manuscript
course she recently taught.

"At the heart of every narrative is contradiction. Don't try to
get rid of it. Write into it."

Then her mind darts back to Oscar's Salon and how stimulating
she finds readers' riffs, creative writing pieces, observations and
critical thinking posted there, yet now she yearns for seclusion.

–3–

Curious. Oscar's taken for a man more frequently in Toronto
than in Vancouver, but with a difference — initial responses are
more power-dynamic-infused, edgy. If someone becomes aware
she's a woman, no apology is issued (frequently is in Vancouver),
which is a relief.

She ponders this as she stands in line waiting for her bank's
ATM and notices how similar ATM machines are to urinals —
how men stand with their legs apart as if at. Watches how both
genders use their bodies to shield their passwords as they would
if their private parts were suddenly exposed in public. Muses on
how stiff bills stick out from the slot into our readied hands.

–4–

Toronto. Oscar's approximation of "going back home." Toronto.
Where Oscar "grew up" as a feminist, writer, lesbian. Traces of
what had passed for her sense of home have all but faded in the
US.

Toronto. Cheryl and Oscar now standing in line for three hours in mid-October full-moon-two-nights-away night. The queue is amicable with anticipation of entering *Kill Joy's Kastle: A Lesbian Feminist Haunted House*. It's performance artist Allyson Mitchell's crowd-source-funded collaboration with twenty-five other lesbian-feminist and queer-fear-fighting artists — a celebratory send-up. As the cold seeps in from the sidewalk, the entrance is finally in sight but still forty-five minutes to go. Oscar jokes that there should be an "Old Gals Fast Lane." Cheryl and Oscar on average thirty plus years older than most others in line.

Halfway through the Haunted House, they turn a corner and there are four lesbians on the floor and one standing. All covered in white cloth except their vaginas, which they display and stroke (one has jewels inside of hers, the one standing uses a mirror). They move their bodies hypnotically, erotically, and some speak, but Oscar is too mesmerized to listen. Too amazed that it has taken her sixty-six years to experience what boys experience and continue to experience throughout their manhood: frequent group displays of their genitals. The bonding in this. Shared intrigue.

Public erotic joy surges through Oscar for the first time.

– 5 –

Oscar. Up late due to sleepless hole in middle of night. Talk with Cheryl over dinner? Conversation on phone last night with Ingrid? Oscar's sense of pacing off: this city is so overstimulating that each additional encounter is amplified. Also — writing mind. When Oscar enters it she finds her capacity for conversation diminishes, sometimes dramatically.

Likely the consult call with Meharoona a factor too. In order to advise her, Oscar needed to read an excerpt of Meharoona's manuscript. Just before bed, Oscar opened the attachment just to get a sense of it. Engrossed, forty minutes later she found she has read the entire excerpt about Meharoona's various accounts of her betweenness.

Then there's this very writing pad itself. Her pen-written letter to her son yesterday has left an intaglio of its entirety on this sheet she now writes upon. Rare manifestation of how their closeness goes underground when he is home with his other mom two provinces away.

– 6 –

Ayelet and Sean's bed cheek by jowl with a large, west-facing window that looks at a small drab-brown brick church with no pretense of grandeur. It seems not to be in use. Upon awakening, Oscar pulls back the curtains each morn to tell the time by where the line between sunshine and shadow is on its façade. On earlier-rising mornings, Oscar watches the sun/ shadow line silently slip from the top of the bell tower down like a theatre curtain reluctantly lowered.

– 7 –

Vertigo. Last night J and Oscar perched in the mythic-sounding Ring 5 of the Four Season Centre, utterly in the grip of "Peter Grimes" for three hours. Britton's score haunting with unusual orchestral interludes between shifts in the opera's action, intensified by a deeply nuanced shadow and light language that so viscerally evoked the gravity of the narrative. Peter Grimes: outsider caught between sea and villagers each as tyrannical as the other. Ultimately there is but one resolution. His only friend instructs him to get in his boat, go out to sea. "Sink her."

Curtain call. Oscar calling out "Bravo!" "Brava!" Final drop of the curtain then the bewilderment of entering hundreds and hundreds of bodies chatting and moving out of the hall down into the subway. J and Oscar staying close, acknowledging how they each want to hold on to what had just happened. Not forget.

– 8 –

Oscar arrives before Eufemia and snags one of the coveted wooden booths in a long-standing haunt of Oscar's, the Queen Mother. They're here to celebrate the release of Eufemia's first book.

A waiter she recognizes from the past arrives at her table.

"Are you waiting for someone?"

> [he has a pronounced black eye that Oscar is trying
> unsuccessfully not to stare at]

Eufemia arrives and Oscar stands to hug her. They exchange "So good to see you(s)" and settle in. The waiter arrives.

> [Oscar notices Eufemia eyeing him]

After he leaves, Oscar offers: "I asked him — it's a black eye from a fight in a bar."

Eufemia smiles ironically. "I didn't think it was a birthmark!"

– 9 –

Eyes closed with pleasure, Oscar basking in the slice of sun angling through kitchen door window having just finished her tea. Opening her eyes she sees a grey squirrel on the southeast corner of the small wooden balcony rail basking too. Its magnificent foot-long tail is wrapped over its back onto its head like an elegant stole that gleams with morning sunlight (as does the squirrel's one eye facing Oscar). Each aware of each. Oscar watches how squirrel's body relaxes as the minutes literally tick by on the kitchen clock. Watches how squirrel too surrenders more and more to the sun until tail slides off body as body softens into full frontal recline — back right leg recklessly splayed in momentary surrender — (inhale, exhale) and gratitude.

– 10 –

— surveillance —

" … espionage dates from the time of the Pharaoh Rameses' war with the Hittites and the battle of Kadesh (c. 1274 BC) … The Hittites king Muwatallis sent two spies into the Egyptian camp posing as defectors … Although most often spies are known as collectors of information, they are often used to disseminate false information in order to deliberately mislead opponents."

The CBC noon news, the Senate in the throes of deciding whether to follow Harper's initiative to kick out his Tory senators Duffy, Wallen and Brazeau or to abide by "presumed innocence," "due process of law" and wait for the RCMP's investigation to conclude. More and more, as the days and debate pass, Harper's "dissemination of false information … to deliberately mislead opponents" becoming more and more apparent.

– 11 –

This waiting unlike any other. Acute attentiveness scanning every sensation and thought for a give-herself-over signal (Oscar's mantra Virginia Woolf's "when the pen gets on the scent"). In her manuscript class, Oscar urging writers to trust the act of sitting (and waiting) or walking (and waiting), not be seduced by every bright, shiny thing. "The narrative is the boss. It knows where it is going. Our job is to follow it and not get in its way."

New York City, 2012. Performance artist Marina Abramović's *The Artist Is Present*. A three-month Museum of Modern Art piece during which she sat for seven hours a day, six days a week and waited. Closed her eyes. Waited. Until the next woman, man or an occasional child sat in the chair opposite her. Then, opened her eyes and met each person's gaze — taking in whatever their eyes expressed — for as long as he or she desired. An endless stream of people waited in line for hours. For this. With her. Their frequent tears for her complete attention sans judgement or expectation, wrenching.

– 12 –

Self-medication. The other day Oscar noticed the big billboard on corner of College and Bathurst advertising Royal Canadian whisky with large block letters:

WHY WAIT

– 13 –

Morality reduced to what you can get away with. Senator Duffy revealing more Harper Conservative caucus lies yesterday. A week ago, Obama maintaining that Merkel's personal cell phone was never tapped by the NSA then two days ago admitted that he knew about it since 2010.

Self-deception the most corrosive of lies — what camouflage hinges on. The logic of lying more tangible, enticing, than the logic of truth. Oscar struck by a psychologist's article in the *New York Times* recently about couples and lying.

Observations that the one who has been lying (debt, addiction, an affair, etc.) for a long time suffers far less than the one who has been deceived once the lies are disclosed. The liar's sense of reality doesn't suddenly crumble nor does she or he feel profoundly betrayed. Also, the liar is not subjected to ongoing blame whereas the deceived one usually is ("You should have realized what was going on; you must have turned a blind eye; you drove him to do it").

We identify with the liar. Disassociate from the one deceived.

"Manipulation of the truth is worse than no truth."

Text from Ai Weiwei's "Self-portrait," 2011

– 14 –

Ai Weiwei's exhbit at the AGO packed. J and Oscar threading their way. Piece after piece draws Oscar close (she can almost hear him breathing next to her), yet he is across the world under house arrest, passport confiscated, guards surrounding him and surveillance cameras everywhere.

Each piece invites. Remnants from destroyed temples sanded to a sheen, stained and stacked into a rectangular arrangement chin-high. His father's artful stacking of their woodpiles inspired him to create elegance from loss and ruin.

The drastic 2008 earthquake. He travels to its epicentre where thousands of school children died as a result of poorly constructed schools. Photographs their backpacks strewn among the rubble. Later, he constructs a snake (suspended from the ceiling) from hundreds of grey backpacks with black and lime green trim fitted together. As Oscar enters, a hushed discomfort lingers overhead.

Halloween. Throughout the day people of all sorts and ages in costume throughout the city, their daily selves and personas replaced by a personality quirk or fantasy that otherwise is subsumed, hidden.

Yesterday, breaking news about Mayor Ford's cover-up being blown open. The missing video of him smoking crack with dealers found via recovery software on a laptop confiscated during an arrest of one of the drug dealers associated with Ford. Momentary elation for those who had suspected it, then, despair: pervasiveness of deception on every level everywhere. Last night, Oscar reading Javier Marias' novel *The Infatuations*:

"I was entirely dependent on him now, for he is the one who decides where to begin and where to end, what to reveal and suggest and keep silent about, when to tell the truth and when to lie or whether to combine the two so that neither is recognizable ... "

Part *34*

Vancouver, Montreal 2014

It. It's not what Oscar imagined after Denis confirmed
she could stay in his apartment while he was away and she
gratefully accepted. She was about to book her flight when
it happened. It had been raining for five days. Then. A rainfall
all through the night pelted Ingrid's peaked ceiling. In the
darkest hour before. Oscar realized Ingrid was stirring: "Are
you awake?" "Yes." "It's such a heavy rain — I think there's
going to be flooding." At breakfast, Oscar mentioned it again.
After returning home and removing her boots, Oscar walked
into the living room and set her foot down into wetness. Her
apartment was flooded. Within a couple of hours after the
restoration team arrived it was evident: her home and office
were uninhabitable. Then. Six weeks of endless calls and emails
squabbling about who did and paid (or wouldn't) for what,
appointments for assessments, meeting various workmen,
retrieving the personal and professional belongings she needed,
finding endless procession of places to stay and work during
the heaviest workload Oscar had ever had.

Much of the expense not covered by insurance. During another
wakeful night she almost decided to give up her Montreal
writing retreat time, then realized how deeply she needed it.
Next morning she asked her brother-in-law, Hoi Sin, if he
would oversee the next phases of the restoration while she was
away. Oscar arranged to do a Montreal consult and workshop
to cover her flight. On the flight: a sore throat: Would she be
able to do the consult? The workshop? She enjoyed both but
then crumpled into a bad cold.

Exhale of relief. She had been caught in the crosshairs of
over thirty pages of tangled email threads with the six men
involved in various aspects of the restoration. Unexplained trade
terminology; curt efforts to snag responsibility onto her or one

another; bullshitting around their mistakes; not paying attention to what's been said, decided, nor sequence the work must be done in nor who must okay what. Underneath it, reluctance to commit anything in writing compounded by corruption of language. The insurance adjuster's trade term "upgrade" (for what in fact was a downgrade) rankles Oscar. "Upgrade" a cover-up: pays for the cheap lino and nylon carpet the developer installed some thirty-eight years before. Oscar. Caught.

Excess of communication = Erosion of comprehension =

Evacuation of conscience.

– 3 –

Montreal. In the darkest hour Oscar abruptly awakens from just having barged into the washroom with blood smeared on the toilet and floor. Crouched in the corner he is gripping the woman. The male customer, who had gone in first, silently stands in other corner his arms sandwiching his body.

It was a new retail store that had an appealing ambience. A few customers were chatting with the store owner couple a few minutes before closing. Amicably, the woman volunteered that an acquaintance (a woman physician) had offered to help finance their start-up. Oscar remarked: "Considering the economic environment these days it's great to hear this kind of support still happens." The woman excused herself and went into the bathroom. Within a minute, her partner abruptly strode over and pushed open the washroom door. Went in.
Silence — sound of the lock — silence.

Scuffling then her odd groan that signalled he had entered her, then increasing sounds of force and agony — everyone in the store frozen in disbelief — then her aching sobs. Silence. Then. Oscar. Went in. Told him:

"Let her go."

– 4 –

After a long period of upheaval and grief, Oscar's apartment had been her refuge these past seven years. The roofers improperly installed inadequate downspouts. Oscar had told the property manager, told the downspout installer that diverting the drainage into flowerbed and patio drain would not work. She was ignored.

– 5 –

Dinner last night. Lise and Oscar talking about Lise's meditation retreat at Auschwitz. The puzzlement about why so few survivors of the death camps would talk about it after they were liberated. Oscar mentions an article she read about the alarming increase of PTSD in US soldiers and how the suicide rate for returning Canadian soldiers has also shot up. In the article, several of the soldiers indicated that few people wanted to hear what they had gone through upon returning home, and that the few who did only wanted to hear about it for a little while. Oscar thinking out loud with Lise: "We judge people who went through the death camps and Second World War for withholding their stories but it's probably apparent to them that hardly anyone could bear to listen."

– 6 –

Oscar. In the new Café Rico on Mont-Royal over cappuccino notices the name and sign in the clothing store window across the street:

MOCHICO
TOUT
50%

Oscar in need of some new trousers (as Ingrid calls them), of which she has too few and almost all are grey. Entering the store, she heads for the men's section downstairs. Oscar has done so ever since she was old enough to shop on her own. Men's clothing styles, fabrics and cuts fit her body better. Too, men's clothing is better made and often less expensive. Here she thinks of her mother and father: how opposite their approaches to clothes shopping were.

Her father shopped at one of the better men's clothiers and over the years had formed a friendship with Bob, a salesman who knew what looked good on her father and would even call her father: "Cy, we've had a shipment of new dress shirts and there is one here that is perfect for you."

On the other hand, Oscar's mother shopped at several stores and routinely would take eight or more dresses home "on trial," hold a fashion show for Oscar and her father to seek their opinion, which she ignored, then routinely returned all the dresses days after they were supposed to be back on the sales floor.

In **MOCHICO**, Oscar quickly looks at trousers, feels fabric. In limited French (Oscar) and English (the clerk), she checks they're 50 percent off. Selects a pair that fits well, pays, walks back to Denis'.

A swatch of burgundy has now entered Oscar's life.

– 7 –
.

Recently, Oscar found herself saying out loud, "I'm my father's best son." She's always known this but been too timid to put it into words.

Put it into words.

A line crossed when we do.

What we say becomes what we see. And don't.

Oscar was uneasy about saying "best son" as it sounded like "better than." This isn't what she means. What she means is that she is most like her father — from having his sneeze to relishing being self-employed.

Free from father-son expectations, Oscar became his best son right under his nose.

Did he ever realize it?

– 8 –

Ingrid and Oscar on the phone acknowledging that they both remain reluctant to talk about their relationship at any length with friends or family. Are still finding their way from a decade of being friends to now being lovers. Each having been single for a long time.

The assumptions about what intimacy is: how to be aware of the assumptions (which suit/which don't). And the assumptions about intimacy their friends and family may have for them.

Putting it in words.

Lines are crossed.

What we say becomes what we see, and don't.

– 9 –

Isn't it all an endless stream of signals emitted in innumerable ways? Of which so much we miss, resist, dismiss?

Oscar tells Lise about the disturbing dream that had abruptly awakened her the previous night. Lise poses the inevitable dream question: "What do you think it was about?" Perhaps it's just about itself, Oscar thinks, yet she senses it was also about her sudden loss of home and office compounded by the feeling of violation as an array of men descended on her refuge every day. Hours each day dealing with it while simultaneously struggling to stay on top of her workload. Yes, that. But more it was the shock. For the first two weeks she didn't want to even go for her daily walk nor to The Drive to shop or have a coffee. Didn't want to run into friends and acquaintances with their innocent, ubiquitous "How are you?" She only went out at night, or on Sunday mornings when she was most unlikely to run into people she knew. Oscar. Shaken. Getting a glimpse of the disorienting force refugees must feel as their life and sense of home is destroyed.

— the velocity of violence —

Its suddenness.
Irreversible speed.

Oscar camped out in Shaye's apartment on the second floor when Shaye was still in Australia for two weeks.

Into Shaye's bedroom, Oscar notices a hand-written letter by a young child on Shaye's chest of drawers.

Dear Dad,

are
We ^ almost having a
flood.

– 12 –

Nancy and Oscar attach cleats to their boots. Nancy wants to show Oscar where she walks along the Saint Lawrence River in Verdun. "It's the only place you can be in nature and walk your dog off leash in Montreal!" Here, the river is sealed over with thick ice, they walk on top of it.

— expanse —

Expanse in their easeful, ranging conversation too. They talk about how Nancy is feeling after her father's death. Then Oscar asks about the sparsely treed island across the river to the south with stark apartment buildings scattered here and there. Nancy tells Oscar it is Nun's Island. Oscar replies, "That's odd because the grey high-rises and sparseness remind me of abject nuns." The island had been lushly forested — magical — when Nancy grew up.

Loss is everywhere.

— thick slab of ice beneath her feet —

Below that? Fierce life flow.

– 13 –

Eastern Ukraine invaded by the Russian army, Crimea rapidly
falling into their control. The Olympic Games now over,
Putin's real game begins. Oscar recalls reading an article in
the *New York Times* a couple of months ago citing two US
presidents' first impression of Putin: George W. Bush saw
compassion in Putin's eyes; Obama saw the eyes of a killer.

– 14 –

Maslow's Hierarchy of Needs surfaced in Oscar's mind
yesterday. Sociology textbook 101. Hadn't thought about it
for decades. The weeks before coming to Montreal, ideas and
images for writing Part 34 were gathering. Oscar didn't note
them down for they always stay afloat in her head. When she
finally began to write last week, most had vanished. It vexed
Oscar until today when Maslow's pyramid diagram resurfaced
in her mind. As a twenty-year-old closet poet and art student,
to see the sequence of human needs so succinctly expressed
had amazed her.

Oscar does a Wikipedia search and sees that at the bottom of
the pyramid are the needs for breathing, food, water, shelter,
clothing, sleep. When these are secured, one moves up to the
next levels of needs. At the pyramid's apex: morality, creativity,
spontaneity, acceptance, purpose, meaning and inner potential.
Oscar's repeated packing up her personal and professional
necessities as she moved between seven temporary locations
prior to Montreal plunged her to the bottom. She takes some
comfort in this for at the bottom nothing is extraneous: a
particular alertness is required. Simplicity.

– 15 –

Her last morning-muse looking out Denis' living room
window, Oscar sips tea as she is absorbed in J. S. Bach's cantatas
82, 102 and 178 that Ingrid gave her. The CD is performed
exquisitely by La Petite Bande. Its title is "Ich Habe Genug"
(I have had enough). This sentiment the antithesis of North
American insatiability. Minutes later, Oscar observes she may, in
fact, be ready to let go of her need for home as den.

– 16 –

To Oscar, the narrative movement in *Oscar of Between* resembles
the longing notes of an Argentine bandoneon — its tango
concertina's repeated squeezing in (intimate) then pulling out
(public) — squeezing in pulling out squeezing close extending
out in a kind of grace.

Part 35

Vancouver, Bath 2015

Two weeks ago Oscar driving on Pacific Avenue heading toward Kate's. It's an elating sunlight-reflected colours fall afternoon. Since she left Ingrid's, Oscar's been glancing at a spider bouncing and twirling with the rush of air repeatedly having to repair its web strung between driver's mirror and car door. For the last few blocks, Oscar's noticed a second, smaller spider that's retreated to the inner lip of the mirror. Is it cowering there? Or, is it smart and just wanting to stay out of the wind?

Then it happens.

The larger one notices it tucked in there. Menace pulses out from it (is Oscar imagining this?). It swings over on a guy strand and lands close to the small one, which immediately darts to the other side — its terror palpable. Oscar wants to intercede but traffic is too heavy — she's caught in the web of this story, gripped by the larger spider's absolute intent to kill radiating from its body. It forcefully swings to the other side of the mirror and the smaller one darts away two more times, its throbbing fear astounding. On the fourth attack, the large one strikes, bites, wraps it, attaches it to the mirror's lip.

Oscar finds a parking spot a few blocks from Kate's, unnerved by what she just watched. Was already feeling vulnerable about attending this informal gathering about "the role of the poet." Oscar, not invited for decades, was surprised to be. Feels a bit like that small spider.

Kate's apartment is full of light and pleasant anticipation. As each poet arrives there's a gathering excitement as this kind of conversation so rarely happens. People help themselves to food and drink, chat, then seem to casually move about as they test who best to position themselves next to.

Once all have alighted, they speak briefly about how each perceive their role as a poet. When the speaking begins, there isn't the typical posturing but rather a probing sincerity. Kate and Renée intentionally invited an array of poets so there's little jockeying and no one group of poets dominates. Oscar resolves to speak as openly as possible; break out of her silence. Her turn. She takes in a deep breath, then begins:

"I stopped writing poetry many years ago (for reasons I won't go into right now) and have been writing lyric prose. That said, whatever I write I write with the mind of a poet; I think like a poet. For me, the poem differs from prose because there's an urgency in its very form. In an essay I wrote years ago for *Breathing the Page*, I say, 'The poem enters your heart like an idea enters your mind.' This urgency shapes how I write lyric prose. For me, my role is to be fully present at the threshold of awe, awe in all its meanings: wonder, dread, reverence and fear."

As the speaking continues, others pick up on what Oscar has said. This surprises her yet she makes no assumptions. Oscar, now at ease with between, is likely never to be among.

– 2 –

Oscar. August 2014, on the Great Western hurtling 120 km/h toward Bath. J and Oscar's son in their assigned seats reading; surfing. Oscar. Standing at the open window between train cars — in unexpected ecstasy — the force of movement and rushing air without impediment or enclosure provokes a state of high alert: pure sensation. Intensified by flashes of copse along the track that speed transforms into pixelated colours.

A few weeks prior, Oscar sitting in a public space with eyes closed when a sudden whoosh rushed over her body: "What was that?" Her eyes bolted open: it was merely a man walking by. Oscar discombobulated. How could she not have been aware of this before? It happens all the time but we become

oblivious to the wake we make. Believe ourselves to be
separate, even "alone."

– 3 –

July 4, 2014. A Moncton, New Brunswick young man in
combat gear walks down the streets and targets RCMP men
killing three.

October 20, 2014. A Saint-Jean-sur-Richelieu young man
targets and runs down two off-duty soldiers, killing one.

October 22, 2014. A Montreal young man walks up to the
Canadian War Memorial and shoots the soldier on duty in the
back, dead, then runs into Parliament where he is shot dead by
a guard.

The massacres and murders by deeply disaffected North
American men mount and mount. As do the gun sales.

February 2015. Although carrying concealed weapons on
campus is banned in forty-one US states, the gun lobby is
fighting back. A Nevada state assemblywoman recently opined:
"If these young, hot little girls on campus have a firearm … the
sexual assaults would go down once these predators get a bullet
in their head."

– 4 –

The *New York Times*, March 8, 2015: "Half the people on the
street are dressed to kill. Every second woman on the avenue
and every second man on the town and every other kid on the
jungle gym has his or her back clad in army green … this year's
models evoke the M-65 field jacket worn by the United States
troops in Vietnam … "

Part 36

Vancouver 2015

– 1 –

Oscar. At ease in her over-stuffed easy chair purchased in a
Toronto used furniture store on The Danforth after emigrating
from US forty years ago. Now, in her already beloved new
fourth floor apartment nest, Oscar gazes at her writing
pad's blank page, then at hemlock, cedar, fir and sequoia at
the foot of her street, then at signature flights of an Anna's
hummingbird, great blue heron, crow. Plum tree just below
extravagantly in bloom for weeks and weeks.

— sunlight illuminates her paper, the white interior walls —

It has been a very long time since. Just now these white walls
arc to Nicole's *The Aerial Letter* that Oscar inhaled in 1988. She
goes to the shelf with Nicole's books on it. Pulls *The Aerial
Letter* off. Opens it and finds the quote so effortlessly it's as if
she had read it yesterday:

"To write, for a lesbian, is to learn how to take down the
patriarchal posters in her room ... to live with bare walls."

– 2 –

Rachel Cusk's *Aftermath: On Marriage and Separation*:

" ... narrative is the aftermath of violent events. It is a means of
reconciling yourself with the past."

The harsh pragmatism of these two sentences. Oscar thinks
of her 1984 book, *open is broken*, recalls her exploration of
"*write*, writan, to tear, scratch" in relation to creating a public
space for lesbian erotic love poems. Oscar and Daphne's books:
combustion.

All forms of combustion create residue; refuse. The question of the matter being whether to re-purpose? Burn, bury? Dump on the defenceless?

"The core of Nazi barbarism, as Levi saw it, was its reduction of unique human beings to anonymous things, mere instances of a collective category — Jews, for example — that can be slaughtered because they have no individual value." The *New York Times Book Review.*

Recently, Oscar becoming aware of how seldom women writers evoke perpetrators (who remain an almost invisible force): perpetrators the narrative territory of men; victims the narrative territory of women. Claudia and Oscar talking about this, sharing an interest in exploring perpetrator violence in their new books.

– 3 –

Gender. What we access, what we don't; what we pay attention to, what we don't; what we value, what we don't. As does race as does class as does sexual preference as does_____ as does_____. If one of these identities happens to be the antithesis of who you know yourself to be, or who you would much rather be, the solution most often is to strive to become the other. This solution usually requires various kinds of deception to "pass" undetected.

Camouflage, simply said, is the act of deceiving in order to do harm. Or, in order to escape harm.

In a recent documentary on transgender and gender reassignment, a male sociologist points out that when we first encounter one another, we must immediately establish which gender each other is for this determines how we speak, what we talk (and do not talk) about and what the acceptable body proximity and body language are. If a person's gender is indeterminate, we are at a complete loss. "Paralyzed."

– 4 –

Panhandlers are the exception. Their acuity for identifying gender is flawless. Is this because, as outsiders, they can ill afford to offend? Or, because they see the posturing and camouflage of people with income is just that? Panhandlers' and Oscar's eyes often meet, sometimes they speak, Oscar frequently gives change (changes — what is needed here).

– 5 –

More and more transgender people are choosing gender reassignment via hormone injections and various types of surgery. It's a relief, often a joyful experience to become the gender one has always felt oneself to be. Mismatched gender can feel like imposed camouflage yet reassignment — in heterosexual society eyes — is often viewed as deception.

Increasingly there is a broader range of identifiers for gender fluidity: Agender, gender neutral, gender queer, non-binary queer and gender non-conforming. Publically affirming the gender spectrum is crucial.

For Oscar, "Not a fitting in. Nor a misfit flaunting out" is who Oscar is. "Even the most aberrant group garrisons its norm; its not between." It has taken Oscar decades to name her betweenness and relish connecting with vast array of other persons of between. In some older cultures, a person of between plays an important role, but not so in North America, except amongst some indigenous peoples.

Gender reassignment. Transitioning from one category's set of expectations to another.

"The loss of position in a white male society is subtle but omnipresent ... I was in a corporate meeting and one of the VPs said, 'Who brought the bagels?' No one had. So the VP says, 'Stephanie, would you mind running out to pick them up?' It was pouring down rain! ... That kind of stuff never happened before I transitioned. It happened all the time after." The *New York Times*, March 8, 2015.

While Americans reluctantly admit "racial bias" exists, they believe they're not racist.

The *New York Times*, January 10, 2015: " ... young black men are shot dead by police at 21 times the rate of young white men."

In Toronto, increasing "incidents" of police shooting and killing of unarmed black men.

A couple of months after this article, there is a mass killing of nine people at one of the oldest black churches in America by a white twenty-one-year-old man who told the minister he wanted to attend their Bible study and prayer meeting.

Language our most devastating camouflage.

Within seconds: categorizing, racial profiling, "Sir" or "Ma'am."
Automatic positioning. What to expect. Who to trust. And not.

Where this takes us.

– 9 –

Oscar reading Claudia Rankine's new book, *Citizen: An
American Lyric*. On the back cover Marjoire Perloff writes:
"These tales of everyday life … dwell on the most normal
exteriors and the most ordinary of daily situations so as to
expose what is really there: a racism so guarded and carefully
masked as to make it all the more insidious."

– 10 –

Category: "*Logic*. Any of the basic classifications into which
all knowledge can be placed. In this sense, also called
'predicament.'"

Category *is* our predicament.

Everyone not in *our* category is a not. This is the knot.

" … photographs of black victims of lynching taken between
the 1880's and 1930's … show Americans grinning beneath
the naked mutilated body of a black man or woman hanging
behind them from a tree. The lynching photographs were
souvenirs of a collective action whose participants felt perfectly
justified in what they had done." The *New York Times*, May 23,
2004.

The "grinning beneath" included children. These "souvenirs"
were widely distributed throughout the US like "Wish You
Were Here" postcards.

– 11 –

Women strangers constantly assuming Oscar is a man:

"So sorry!"

"Oh, pardon me."

"Sorry, you should go first."

It's staggering.

Staggering, when you stop to consider the implications of one category of people constantly having to apologize, give way to, another category of people. Apologizing their whole life.
Category, camouflage, cruelty
: the co-dependent relationship among them.

Endless categories in which one individual or group must unfailingly be subservient to another.

– 12 –

Oscar and Darrel are having lunch and talking about their manuscripts and histories with betweenness. Oscar tells Darrel her betweenness began in childhood but she didn't know how to express it then. Says, when she became a writer, her betweenness gradually came more into focus with her subject matter and lack of inclusion. As she developed her style of blending poetic strategies, exploration of ideas and narrative prose she grew to accept her solitariness. In telling this story, she found her narrative position: a person of between. Oscar finally isn't obliged to category and its attendant allegiances. Isn't at the mercy of its exclusions.

Darrel gets it. He talks about various aspects of his life as a Cree man and how in Oscar's class, he discovered he's a writer.

– 13 –

"It is only when one crosses a limit or a boundary that certain words are enunciated with clarity."

— Najwa Ali, *Writing Toward a Distance*

– 14 –

Oscar. Dwelling between urban apartment buildings and Stanley Park's 1,000 acres of rainforest held by the sea.

For the first few weeks, Oscar and Ingrid take frequent long walks on the park's trails then wander more and more off trail.

Off trail, it's immediate.

– 15 –

It's immediate. Categories of groomed trails, park map in hand and safety-maintained trees on either side give way to nature's fervent instinct to survive, thrive, endlessly reinvent, redefine itself.

– 16 –

— in this here of between Oscar resides —

Acknowledgements

My sincere thank-you to the editors who have published excerpts of *Oscar of Between*. Excerpts in anthologies have appeared in *Alone Together; Kwe: Standing With Our Sisters; Planet Earth Poetry Anthology*, and *The Tolerance Project*. Journals that have published excerpts have included *CV2, Plenitude*, and *Dandelion*. In addition, my interactive Oscar's Salon, at www.betsywarland.com, is proving to be a fascinating experience and continues to spur me on. Brava and bravo to all my Guest Writers and Artists, and readers who post their lively comments. I am indebted to the skill, commitment and creativity of my web, social media and editing team of Zsuzsi Huebsch, John Gardiner, Marial Shea and Lindsay Glauser Kwan.

Gratitude is the only word for a Canada Council writing grant and the jury members who believed in this manuscript.

Given that my full-time office and meeting space is housed in my small apartment, concentrated writing time has been hard to elbow out. Over the years, apartment and house sits enabled a number of writing retreats that have been absolutely crucial. Denis Lessard, Maxine Young, Clarissa Green and Ayelet Tsabari — I kiss your feet.

There should be more words for "thank you"!

Deep appreciation to my writing and artist friends who followed my nine-year Oscar quest via our conversations and your reading parts of the manuscript: your companionship made all the difference.

Barbara Kuhne has been my editor for three of my nonfiction books (*Proper Deafinitions; Breathing the Page: Reading the Act of Writing; Oscar of Between*). Her remarkable range of editing skills and ability to understand each of these books has been, quite simply, invaluable.

Too, after twenty-five years, I am delighted to be publishing in British Columbia again and doubly delighted to be publishing with the dynamic publisher Caitlin Press, and have *Oscar of Between* in the launch of their new imprint, Dagger Editions.

Sources

Ali, Najwa. *Writing Toward a Distance*

Anonymous. *A Woman in Berlin*

Artblart.cm, tagged 'ai weiwie self-portrait

Bakewell, Sarah. *How to Live — Or a Life of Montaigne in One Question and Twenty Attempts at an Answer*

Brossard, Nicole. *The Aerial Letter*

Cusk, Rachel. *Aftermath: On Marriage and Separation*

Hillman, Brenda. *The Grand Permission: New Writing on Poetics and Motherhood*

Leggett, John. *Ross and Tom: Two American Tragedies*

Lispector, Clarice. *The Passion According to G.H.*

Marías, Javier. *The Infatuations*

Newark, Tim. *Camouflage* [Thames & Hudson, exhibit book]

Ramana Rao, J.V. *Introduction to Camouflage and Deception*

Rankine, Claudia. *Citizen: An American Lyric*

Rich, Adrienne. *The Dream of a Common Language*

Rich, Adrienne. *Twenty-One Love Poems*

Rybczynski, Witold. *Home: A Short History of an Idea*

Tanasescu, Chris. Margento [http://christanasescu.blogspot.ca/]

Woolf, Virginia. *A Writer's Diary*

Woolf, Virginia. *Orlando*.

This book is set in Bembo. Based on a design cut around 1495 by Francesco Griffo for printer Aldus Manutius, Bembo is an old style type face and was revived by Monotype Corporation in 1929.

The text was typeset by Vici Johnstone.

Caitlin Press, Spring 2016.